Website Building Granny

Dedication

This book is dedicated to all the curious minds out there, especially those who may feel a little intimidated by technology. You're never too old, or too new to the digital world, to learn and build something amazing. This is for all the grandmas, grandpas, and anyone who wants to take control of their online presence and share their stories, passions, and ideas with the world. Let's build some websites!

Preface

Welcome to "Website Building Granny," a friendly guide designed to empower you to build your own website, even if you've never touched a line of code before. I remember when I first started exploring the world of websites, it felt like a whole new language. But with a little patience, a lot of curiosity, and some helpful guidance, I realized anyone can create a fantastic online space.

This book is born from my passion for sharing my knowledge and making technology accessible to everyone. Whether you're a retiree wanting to start a blog, a small business owner looking to expand your reach, or simply someone who wants to express themselves online, this guide will walk you through every step of the process.

We'll cover everything from choosing the perfect domain name and hosting provider to designing your website, creating engaging content, and promoting your work. I'll be your virtual guide, offering practical tips, troubleshooting advice, and real-life examples to help you along the way. So, grab a cup of tea (or a glass of wine!), get comfortable, and let's embark on this exciting journey together.

Introduction

In today's digital world, having an online presence is more important than ever. Whether you're a passionate hobbyist, a small business owner, or simply someone who wants to share your thoughts and stories with the world, a website can be your digital doorway to success.
But the idea of building a website can be daunting, especially for those who aren't familiar with web development. You might be thinking:
"I'm not tech-savvy, how can I possibly do this?"
"Is this something only younger people can do?"
"I don't have any coding experience, will this be too difficult for me?"
Let me assure you, building a website is not as complicated as it might seem. With the right guidance, even a "granny" like me can master the basics and create a beautiful, functional website!
In this book, I'll guide you through the entire process of website building, from the initial brainstorming to launching your website and beyond. You'll learn about:
Planning your website: Defining your goals, researching your audience, and choosing the right domain name and hosting provider.
Choosing the perfect platform: Exploring different website builders and diving into the world of WordPress, a powerful yet user-friendly option.
Setting up your website: Walking through the installation process, customizing your design, and adding essential features like plugins.
Creating captivating content: Learning how to write engaging blog posts, incorporate images and videos, and use SEO to get your website noticed.

Expanding your reach: Discovering effective marketing strategies, utilizing email marketing, and building a strong online community.

This book is designed to be your friendly guide, offering clear explanations, practical examples, and troubleshooting tips to help you navigate the world of website building with confidence. So, whether you're just starting your online journey or looking to refine your existing website, let's get started!

Understanding Your Website Goals

Before you embark on this exciting journey of building your very own website, it's crucial to take a moment to reflect on what you hope to achieve. Imagine your website as a cozy cottage you're building from scratch. Before you start laying the foundation, you need a clear vision of what kind of home you want to create. Do you envision a cozy retreat nestled amidst a flower garden, a bustling farmhouse with a welcoming porch, or a modern, minimalist abode? Just like a home, your website should reflect your unique personality and purpose.

Think of your website as your digital footprint, your online presence, and your window to the world. It's your opportunity to connect with others, share your passions, showcase your talents, or even build a thriving online business. So, what do you want your website to accomplish? Are you dreaming of:

Sharing your passions with the world? Perhaps you're a talented artist, a passionate gardener, or an avid traveler. A website allows you to create a virtual space where you can share your experiences, insights, and creative endeavors with a global audience.
Building a community around your interests? Do you have a love for vintage cars, a knack for knitting, or a passion for cooking? Your website can become a hub for like-minded individuals to connect, share ideas, and learn from each other.
Promoting your business or service? Whether you're a freelance writer, a small business owner, or a musician, a website is an essential tool to showcase your offerings, attract potential clients, and grow your brand.

Connecting with friends and family? Even if you're not looking to build a massive online presence, a website can be a fantastic way to stay connected with loved ones, share family photos, or announce important milestones.

Defining Your Goals:

Now, let's delve into the process of defining your website goals. Think of this as creating a roadmap for your online journey. The more specific and actionable your goals, the clearer your path will become. Here's a framework to help you:

What do you want to achieve with your website? Think of this as your overall objective. Do you want to build a personal brand, generate leads for your business, or create a platform for sharing your knowledge?
Who is your target audience? Identifying your ideal visitors is crucial for creating content they'll find engaging and valuable. Who are you trying to reach with your website? What are their interests, needs, and pain points?
What are your website's key features? What aspects of your website will contribute to achieving your goals? Will it include a blog, a portfolio, an e-commerce store, or a contact form?
How will you measure success? Establishing key performance indicators (KPIs) will help you track your website's progress and make adjustments as needed. Will you measure success based on website traffic, lead generation, or sales?

Examples of Clear Website Goals:

Let's bring these concepts to life with some real-world examples:

Goal: To establish a personal brand as a freelance writer.
Target audience: Businesses and individuals seeking high-quality writing services.
Key features: Portfolio showcasing past work, blog with insightful articles on writing, and a contact form for inquiries.
Success metrics: Website traffic, lead generation through contact form, and client inquiries.

Goal: To build a community of dog lovers and share tips on dog training.
Target audience: Dog owners seeking information and support.
Key features: Blog with dog training articles, forum for discussions, and a section for sharing dog photos.
Success metrics: Website traffic, active forum users, and engagement on social media.

Goal: To sell handmade jewelry online.
Target audience: Individuals interested in unique and handcrafted jewelry.
Key features: E-commerce store with product descriptions and high-quality images, blog with design inspiration, and social media integration.
Success metrics: Website traffic, sales conversion rate, and social media engagement.

The Power of Clarity:

Defining clear website goals provides numerous benefits:

Focus and direction: It helps you stay focused on your vision and make informed decisions throughout the website development process.
Content strategy: It guides your content creation and ensures that it aligns with your target audience's interests.

Marketing efforts: It allows you to develop targeted marketing campaigns that reach the right people.
Website design: It influences the design and layout of your website, making it user-friendly and appealing to your target audience.
Success measurement: It provides a framework for tracking your website's progress and making necessary adjustments.

Your Website's Journey Begins:

Now that you have a better understanding of the importance of defining your website goals, it's time to begin your journey. Don't be afraid to dream big and let your imagination run wild. Remember, your website is a reflection of your passions, your expertise, and your vision for the future. By setting clear goals and staying focused, you'll be well on your way to creating a website that truly represents you and achieves your online aspirations.

Researching Your Target Audience

Imagine a bustling marketplace, filled with diverse vendors showcasing their wares. You, as a website owner, are one of these vendors, and your website is your virtual storefront. To attract customers, you need to understand who your ideal customers are and what they're looking for. This is where researching your target audience comes in.

Think of your target audience as your dream customers. They're the people who are most likely to be interested in your website's content, products, or services. To discover who they are, ask yourself questions like:

What are their demographics? This includes their age, gender, location, education level, income, and occupation. Understanding these demographics helps you paint a picture of your ideal customer.

What are their interests and hobbies? What kind of content do they enjoy reading or watching? What kind of products or services are they interested in? Understanding their interests helps you tailor your website's content to their needs.

What are their online habits? Do they prefer to browse on their computers or smartphones? What social media platforms do they use? Knowing their online habits helps you reach them effectively.

What are their pain points? What are their biggest challenges or frustrations? How can your website help them overcome these challenges? Addressing their pain points is crucial for establishing trust and building a loyal audience.

Here are some practical ways to research your target audience:

Use Google Analytics: Google Analytics is a free tool that provides valuable insights into your website visitors. It tells you where your visitors are coming from, what pages they visit, how long they stay on your site, and much more. This data can help you identify your core audience and understand their behavior.

Conduct surveys: Create a simple survey to collect feedback from your existing or potential customers. Ask questions about their demographics, interests, and what they're looking for in a website. You can use online survey tools like SurveyMonkey or Google Forms to create and distribute your surveys.

Analyze your competitors: Look at your competitors' websites and social media pages to see who they're targeting and what content they're producing. This can give you valuable insights into your own target audience and how to differentiate yourself.

Engage with your audience: Interact with your followers on social media, respond to comments on your blog posts, and ask for feedback on your website. This helps you build relationships and gather valuable insights.

Crafting Your Website's Voice:

Once you've identified your target audience, it's time to craft your website's voice. This refers to the tone and style of your website's content. Think of it as the personality of your website.

Consider these factors when crafting your voice:

Formal vs. Informal: Are you aiming for a professional and formal tone or a more casual and conversational style?

Serious vs. Humorous: Do you want to come across as serious and authoritative or more lighthearted and engaging?

Technical vs. Simple: Will your content be technical and jargon-filled or easy to understand for a broader audience?

Target audience: Remember, your voice should resonate with your target audience. For example, if you're targeting a younger audience, you might use slang or emojis, while a more mature audience might prefer a more formal tone.

Here are some tips for crafting your website's voice:

Use consistent language: Ensure that your writing style is consistent throughout your website. This includes using a consistent tone, grammar, and punctuation.

Use clear and concise language: Avoid using jargon or technical terms that your audience might not understand. Keep your sentences short and to the point.

Use storytelling: People connect with stories. Incorporate storytelling elements into your website's content to make it more engaging and memorable.

Use humor sparingly: Humor can be a great way to connect with your audience, but use it sparingly and ensure it's appropriate for your target audience.

Get feedback: Ask friends, family, or colleagues to read your website's content and provide feedback on its tone and style.

Beyond the Basics: Understanding Customer Personas

For a more in-depth understanding of your target audience, consider creating customer personas. These are fictional representations of your ideal customers, based on your research and insights.

Here are some elements to include in your customer personas:

Name and photo: Give your persona a name and a picture to help you visualize them.

Demographics: Include their age, gender, location, education level, income, and occupation.

Interests and hobbies: Outline their interests, hobbies, and online habits.

Goals and aspirations: What are their hopes and dreams? What are they trying to achieve?

Pain points and challenges: What are their biggest frustrations or challenges? How can your website help them?

Quotes and anecdotes: Include quotes or anecdotes that capture their personality and voice.

Benefits of Customer Personas:

Focus your marketing efforts: By understanding your ideal customers, you can target them with more relevant and effective marketing messages.

Create more engaging content: Knowing your customer's needs and interests helps you create content that is more relevant and engaging for them.

Improve website design: You can design your website to cater to the needs and preferences of your target audience.

Make better decisions: Customer personas can help you make informed decisions about your website's content, design, and marketing strategy.

Remember, understanding your target audience is crucial for website success. By taking the time to research and understand your ideal customers, you can create a website that resonates with them, builds trust, and ultimately, achieves your website goals.

Choosing the Right Domain Name

Ah, the domain name—the digital address of your website, the first impression you make on the internet. It's like picking a name for your baby (or maybe your pet!), but with a little more emphasis on practicality. A good domain name is memorable, relevant to your website's content, and easy to type and remember.

Imagine it like this: your website is your online home, and the domain name is your street address. You want a street address that's easy to find, makes sense for your home, and isn't already taken by someone else!

Finding the Perfect Domain Name: A Treasure Hunt

So, how do you go about finding the perfect domain name? It's a bit like a treasure hunt, but don't worry, I'll be your trusty guide!

First, you need to brainstorm. Think about your website's content. What are you trying to achieve with your website? If you're selling handmade jewelry, you might want a name that reflects that. If you're a travel blogger, maybe a name that evokes adventure and wanderlust is right for you.

Once you've got a few ideas, try out different variations. Is your name too long or too short? Does it include any keywords that are important to your website's content? Try combining different words to create a catchy and memorable name. Don't be afraid to get creative!

Don't Forget the Basics:

Keep it short and sweet: A catchy and short domain name is easier to remember and share.
Make it easy to spell and pronounce: No one wants to struggle to type your domain name!
Choose a relevant name: Your domain name should reflect the content of your website.
Check for availability: Before you get too attached to a name, make sure it's not already taken!

Some Handy Tips:

Think about your target audience: Who are you trying to reach with your website? Consider their interests and how they might search for information related to your website.
Use keyword research: This can help you identify relevant keywords to include in your domain name. There are free tools available online that can help you with this.
Avoid hyphens: These can make your domain name look cluttered and harder to remember.
Consider using a memorable acronym: If your website is for an organization or business, a catchy acronym might be a good option.
Look for available extensions: The most common extension is .com, but there are many others to choose from, such as .net, .org, and .info.

Don't Be Afraid to Get Creative!

Remember, your domain name is your first impression on the internet. It should be memorable, relevant, and easy to find. Use your creativity and have fun with it! And if you're still feeling lost, don't hesitate to ask me for help.

Now, let's talk about finding a trustworthy web hosting service. This is where your website actually lives, so you want to choose a provider that's reliable and has excellent customer support. Think of it like finding the perfect neighborhood for your online home!

Understanding Web Hosting Basics

Now that you have chosen a catchy domain name, it's time to find a cozy home for your website – a web host! Imagine it as a virtual apartment where your website can reside and be accessed by everyone in the online world. Just like a landlord takes care of the building, a web host provides the necessary space, resources, and infrastructure for your website to operate smoothly.

Think of web hosting as the backbone of your online presence. It's the foundation upon which your entire website rests. Without reliable web hosting, your website might face challenges like slow loading times, frequent downtime, or even worse, disappear from the internet altogether.

To understand the basics of web hosting, let's break it down into simple terms:

1. Web Hosting Explained

Imagine you're writing a letter to a friend. You need an envelope to hold the letter and a postal service to deliver it to your friend's address. Similarly, when you build a website, you need a web host to store all the files that make up your website (like the letter) and to deliver those files to visitors (like the postal service).

Web hosting companies provide dedicated servers, which are powerful computers specifically designed to host websites. These servers are connected to the internet, allowing visitors from all over the world to access your website.

2. Types of Web Hosting

There are different types of web hosting, each suited to different needs and budgets. Understanding these options can help you choose the best fit for your website:

Shared Hosting: This is like living in a shared apartment – you share the resources of a server with other websites. It's usually the most affordable option, perfect for small personal websites or blogs with low traffic.

VPS Hosting: Think of this as a semi-detached house. You get your own dedicated space on a shared server, offering more resources and control than shared hosting. It's suitable for websites with moderate traffic and those requiring more advanced features.

Dedicated Hosting: Imagine having your own mansion. You get an entire server dedicated solely to your website, providing maximum power, speed, and security. This option is best for high-traffic websites, demanding applications, or e-commerce platforms.

Cloud Hosting: This is like living in a flexible, scalable apartment complex. Your website is hosted across a network of servers, offering flexibility, scalability, and high availability. It's ideal for websites with unpredictable traffic spikes and those needing to easily expand their resources.

3. Choosing the Right Web Host

Selecting the right web host is crucial for your website's success. Here are key factors to consider:

Reliability: Choose a host known for uptime and minimal downtime. A website that's constantly unavailable will quickly lose visitors and credibility.

Speed: A slow-loading website can drive visitors away. Look for a host that offers fast server speeds and resources to ensure a smooth browsing experience.

Customer Support: You'll need help from time to time. Ensure the host offers responsive and helpful customer support, available via email, phone, or live chat.

Features: Consider the features offered by the host, such as database support, email accounts, security features, and backups.

Security: Your website's security is paramount. Choose a host with robust security measures to protect your data and prevent attacks.

Pricing: Compare prices and packages from different hosts. Consider your budget and the features you need. Remember, the cheapest option might not always be the best value for money.

4. Top Web Hosting Providers

Numerous reputable web hosting providers offer various services and features. Here are a few popular options:

Bluehost: A popular choice for beginners, offering affordable plans and excellent customer support.

HostGator: Known for its reliability and wide range of hosting options, including shared, VPS, and dedicated hosting.

GoDaddy: A well-known provider with a vast range of services, including domain registration, web hosting, and website builders.

DreamHost: Focuses on user-friendly hosting solutions, including shared, VPS, and cloud hosting.

SiteGround: Highly regarded for its speed, performance, and excellent customer support.

5. Setting Up Your Web Hosting Account

Once you've chosen a provider, setting up your web hosting account is relatively straightforward. Here's a general process:

Sign Up: Visit the web host's website, select a plan, and provide the necessary information.

Choose a Plan: Choose the plan that best fits your needs and budget.

Domain Name: If you haven't already, you can register a domain name through the host or transfer an existing one.

Account Setup: Follow the instructions provided by the host to set up your account and access your control panel.

Install WordPress: If you're using WordPress, the host usually offers one-click installation for easy setup.

6. Understanding Web Hosting Terminology

Here's a glossary of common web hosting terms you might encounter:

Bandwidth: The amount of data that can be transferred to and from your website in a given time period.

Disk Space: The storage space on the server allocated for your website's files.

Uptime: The percentage of time your website is available online.

Downtime: The time your website is unavailable.

Control Panel: An online interface where you can manage your web hosting account, including website files, databases, email accounts, and more.

FTP (File Transfer Protocol): A protocol used to transfer files between your computer and the web server.

SSL Certificate: A security certificate that encrypts data transmitted between your website and visitors, ensuring secure communication.

cPanel: A popular control panel used by many web hosting providers, offering a user-friendly interface for managing your website.

Conclusion

Choosing the right web host and setting up your hosting account is a crucial step in your website building journey. It's like finding the perfect foundation for your online home. By considering the factors outlined above, you can ensure your website has a solid and reliable foundation for growth and success. Remember, a good web host is a valuable partner in your online ventures, providing the essential support you need to build and maintain a thriving website.

Setting Up Your Hosting Account

Now that you've chosen a domain name, it's time to find a place for your website to live – a web hosting service. Think of it like renting a virtual home for your website. Just like you wouldn't want to live in a cramped, unreliable house, you need a reliable and spacious web hosting provider to keep your website running smoothly and accessible to everyone.

Web hosting is like renting a space on a powerful computer that can handle all the traffic to your website. This computer is located in a data center – a secure, climate-controlled facility designed to keep all those website files safe and humming along.

To find the perfect web hosting provider, you'll need to consider a few key factors:

1. Shared Hosting: The Budget-Friendly Option

Shared hosting is like living in a shared apartment – several websites share the same server resources. This is the most affordable option, perfect for beginners and personal websites with moderate traffic.

2. VPS Hosting: Stepping Up the Power

VPS hosting is like renting a standalone apartment. You have your own dedicated space on the server, offering more control and resources than shared hosting. This is suitable for websites with growing traffic or those needing more flexibility.

3. Dedicated Hosting: The Ultimate Luxury

Dedicated hosting is like owning a mansion! You have an entire server all to yourself, providing the ultimate performance and security. This is ideal for high-traffic websites, e-commerce sites, or those requiring specific configurations.

4. Cloud Hosting: Scalability and Flexibility

Cloud hosting is like living in a network of interconnected apartments. Your website's data is spread across multiple servers, making it incredibly reliable and scalable. It's a great choice for businesses that experience fluctuating traffic or need to quickly scale their website resources.

Choosing the Right Plan

Once you've decided on the type of hosting, it's time to pick a hosting plan that fits your needs and budget. Think of it as selecting a rental plan for your virtual home. Hosting plans vary in terms of storage space, bandwidth, and features. Consider your website's expected traffic volume and resources needed to make an informed choice.

Key Features to Consider

Storage Space: How much data can you store on your website? This includes website files, images, videos, and databases.
Bandwidth: How much data can your website transfer per month? This is important for handling traffic and website loading speeds.
Database Storage: How much space do you need for your website's database? Databases store information like user details, blog posts, and product inventory.

Email Accounts: How many email accounts do you need for your website? Many hosting plans offer email services with your domain name.

Security Features: Does the hosting provider offer security measures like malware protection, firewalls, and daily backups?

A Word on Free Hosting

While tempting, free hosting services often come with limitations and limitations, like advertising on your website or limited resources. They're a good starting point if you're just experimenting, but they may not be suitable for a serious website.

Setting Up Your Hosting Account

Now it's time to get your hosting account up and running! This is like moving into your virtual apartment. The process typically involves:

1. Choosing a Hosting Provider

Do Your Research: Explore popular hosting providers like Bluehost, HostGator, GoDaddy, DreamHost, and SiteGround. Read reviews, compare prices, and consider their customer support options.

Check for Features and Plans: Make sure they offer the type of hosting you need (shared, VPS, dedicated, or cloud) and a plan that aligns with your budget and requirements.

2. Signing Up for a Plan

Select a Plan: Choose the hosting plan that best suits your needs and budget.

Provide Account Information: Enter your personal information, billing details, and payment method.
Create a Password: Choose a strong password to secure your hosting account.

3. Setting Up Your Account

Access Your Control Panel: Your hosting provider will provide you with access to a web-based control panel, like cPanel or Plesk. This is your central hub for managing your website's files, databases, email accounts, and other settings.
Create a Database: If you plan to use a database-driven website (like WordPress), you'll need to create a database in your control panel.
Configure Security Settings: Set up passwords for your database and other sensitive information.

4. Installing WordPress (if Applicable)

Find the WordPress Installer: Most hosting providers have a one-click WordPress installer within their control panel.
Enter Website Information: Provide your domain name, database information, and administrative username and password.
Complete the Installation: Follow the on-screen instructions to complete the WordPress installation.

5. Accessing Your Website

Open Your Website: Once the installation is complete, you can access your website by typing your domain name into your web browser.
Log in to WordPress: Use your administrative username and password to access the WordPress dashboard, where you can start creating and managing your website's content.

Tips for a Smooth Setup

Keep Your Password Secure: Use a strong, unique password for your hosting account and database.

Backup Regularly: Make sure to back up your website files and database periodically to avoid data loss.

Read the Documentation: Familiarize yourself with your hosting provider's documentation and support resources.

Contact Support if Needed: Don't hesitate to reach out to your hosting provider's customer support team if you encounter any issues.

A Few Final Thoughts

Choosing the right hosting provider and setting up your account is an essential step in your website journey. It lays the foundation for a successful website. Remember, the world of hosting can be complex, but don't be intimidated. Take your time, do your research, and seek help when needed. With a little patience and effort, you'll have your website hosted and ready to share with the world.

Exploring Website Builders

Okay, let's dive into the exciting world of website builders. Just like choosing the right tools for your favorite hobby, picking the right platform for your website is crucial for success.

Imagine you're setting up a bake sale. Do you want a fancy, customizable stand where you can arrange everything just so, or would you prefer a simple, pre-made booth with limited options? Website builders are similar – they offer different levels of control and features.

Some popular options include Wix, Squarespace, GoDaddy, and Weebly. Each has its own personality, strengths, and weaknesses.

Wix: The Creative Canvas

Think of Wix as a blank canvas for your artistic vision. It's known for its drag-and-drop interface, making it easy to move elements around like puzzle pieces. Wix offers tons of pre-designed templates that can give you a head start, but you can also go wild with customization. It's perfect for those who want a unique look and feel, even if they aren't tech-savvy.

Pros:

Intuitive Drag-and-Drop: It's like playing with virtual building blocks, making it easy to create a layout that fits

your style.
Stunning Templates: Wix offers a vast library of templates, from sleek and modern to playful and quirky.
Mobile-Friendly: Wix ensures your site looks great on all devices, so your visitors have a smooth experience regardless of their screen size.

Cons:

Limited Customization: While Wix allows for flexibility, some advanced features require coding knowledge.
Can Be Expensive: Wix's free plan has limitations, and premium plans can get pricey, especially for larger websites with lots of features.
Switching Templates Can Be Tricky: Once you choose a template, switching can be complicated, so think carefully before committing.

Squarespace: The Stylish Choice

Squarespace is like a magazine editor for your website. It's all about elegant design and making your site look polished and professional. Their templates are curated for style and are perfect for showcasing your brand.

Pros:

Beautiful, Minimalist Templates: Squarespace is known for its sleek and sophisticated templates, perfect for brands looking for a clean, modern look.
Easy to Use: Their interface is user-friendly, making it simple to manage content and create a visually appealing site.

Built-in SEO Features: Squarespace makes it easy to optimize your website for search engines, helping more people find you.

Cons:

Less Customizable: While Squarespace offers templates with some customization options, it's not as flexible as Wix for truly unique designs.
Limited Feature Set: Some advanced features, like e-commerce, may require additional plugins, which can add to the cost.
Can Be Pricey: Like Wix, Squarespace offers a free plan, but its limitations may require you to upgrade to a paid plan to get the full experience.

GoDaddy: The Established Name

GoDaddy is like the seasoned veteran of website builders. It's a familiar name with a wide range of options and a strong reputation for hosting.

Pros:

Wide Range of Options: GoDaddy offers everything from simple personal websites to complex e-commerce stores.
Reliable Hosting: GoDaddy is known for its reliable hosting, ensuring your website stays up and running smoothly.
Easy-to-Use Website Builder: Their website builder is user-friendly, making it easy to create a basic website even if you're a novice.

Cons:

Templates Can Be Outdated: While GoDaddy has plenty of templates, some can feel a bit dated compared to newer website builders.
Limited Customization: GoDaddy's customization options may not be as flexible as other builders, especially for those looking for unique designs.
Can Be Expensive: Their premium plans can be costly, especially for large websites with extensive features.

Weebly: The Beginner-Friendly Option

Weebly is like your friendly neighborhood website builder. It's simple, straightforward, and great for those who want to get their website up and running quickly without a lot of fuss.

Pros:

Easy-to-Use Interface: Weebly's drag-and-drop interface makes it super easy to build a website without needing any technical expertise.
Free Plan Available: You can create a basic website for free, which is ideal for testing the waters before committing to a paid plan.
Mobile-Optimized: Weebly ensures your website looks great on all devices, including smartphones and tablets.

Cons:

Limited Templates: Weebly's template library is smaller than some other builders, and some designs can be a bit

basic.
Fewer Advanced Features: Weebly may not be the best choice if you're looking for advanced features like e-commerce or complex website integrations.
Basic Customization Options: While Weebly offers some customization options, it's not as flexible as other builders for creating unique designs.

Finding the Right Fit:

Choosing the right website builder depends on your needs and preferences. Ask yourself these questions:

How much control do you want over your website's design?
What are your website's primary goals?
What's your budget?
What level of technical expertise do you have?

Don't be afraid to experiment. Many builders offer free trials or free plans, so you can get a feel for their interface and see if they meet your expectations. Just remember, like baking a delicious cake, finding the right ingredients and tools is the key to a successful website!

Introduction to WordPress

Imagine you've got a fantastic idea for a website, maybe a blog about your favorite recipes, a portfolio showcasing your photography, or an online shop selling your handmade crafts. You're ready to dive in, but where do you start? There are many website platforms out there, each with its own strengths and weaknesses. In Chapter 1, we explored the importance of choosing a domain name and hosting service. Now, it's time to decide on the platform that will be the foundation of your website.

One of the most popular and versatile options is **WordPress**. Think of it as a digital toolkit that provides everything you need to build and manage your website, even if you've never touched a line of code before. WordPress is like a blank canvas, ready to be transformed into the website of your dreams.

Why is WordPress such a popular choice, you ask? It's like the Swiss Army Knife of website platforms. Here are a few key reasons why WordPress might be perfect for you:

User-Friendly: WordPress is designed to be accessible to everyone, even if you're a tech newbie. Its intuitive interface allows you to create content, customize designs, and add functionality without needing extensive technical knowledge. Think of it like putting together a simple puzzle, each piece fitting perfectly into place.

Flexibility and Customization: WordPress is remarkably flexible, allowing you to create a website that truly reflects your unique vision. With a vast library of free and premium themes, you can easily change the look and feel of your site to match your brand or personal style. It's like having a wardrobe full of different outfits, ready to be chosen for any occasion. Furthermore, WordPress is highly customizable. You can add different features and functionalities through plugins, giving you complete control over your website's functionality. Imagine having a toolbox full of handy tools for creating the perfect website.

Community and Support: WordPress boasts a huge and active community of users and developers, ready to lend a hand. If you encounter any challenges or have questions, you're sure to find helpful resources and support online. It's like having a friendly neighborhood group always ready to offer a helping hand.

SEO-Friendly: WordPress is built with search engine optimization (SEO) in mind, making it easier for your website to be found by potential visitors. You'll learn how to optimize your website to rank higher in search engine results, attracting more visitors and growing your online presence. Imagine your website as a beacon, shining brightly and attracting visitors from all corners of the internet.

Scalability: Whether you're starting small or planning to grow your website into a large online presence, WordPress can handle it. It's a scalable platform, accommodating your needs as your website evolves. Think of it as a sturdy tree, growing strong and adaptable over time.

Open Source: WordPress is an open-source platform, which means it's free to use and modify. You don't have to pay any licensing fees, and you're free to customize it to your heart's content. It's like having a free and open-source recipe for a delicious website, ready to be customized and enjoyed by everyone.

Imagine you're embarking on a grand adventure to build your very own website. WordPress is like your trusty companion, providing the tools, support, and flexibility you need to create something truly special.

Now, let's delve deeper into the specifics of using WordPress. You might be wondering, "Is WordPress.com the same as WordPress.org?" The answer is a resounding "not quite." Both platforms are powered by WordPress, but there are some key differences that might influence your decision.

WordPress.com is a hosted platform, similar to using a website builder like Wix or Squarespace. You don't have to worry about technical details like hosting or domain names. WordPress.com takes care of all that for you. It's like having a ready-made website package, complete with all the bells and whistles.

WordPress.org , on the other hand, is self-hosted. This means you'll need to handle the technical aspects of hosting and domain names. Think of it as a more flexible and customizable DIY approach to website building.

So, which is better? The choice depends on your needs and comfort level. If you prefer a simpler, more hands-off approach, WordPress.com is a great option. However, if you're looking for ultimate flexibility, control, and customization, WordPress.org is the way to go.

Let's break down the key differences between these two platforms to help you make an informed decision.

WordPress.com

Pros:
Easy to set up and use.

No technical knowledge required.
Affordable plans for various needs.
Built-in features for security and maintenance.
Large and active community.

Cons:
Limited customization options compared to WordPress.org.
Some features may require paid plans.
You don't have complete control over your website's code.

WordPress.org

Pros:
Unlimited customization potential.
Access to a vast library of free and premium themes and plugins.
Full control over your website's code and data.
Suitable for large, complex websites.

Cons:
Requires technical knowledge for setup and maintenance.
You'll need to manage hosting and security yourself.
Potentially more expensive than WordPress.com.

Remember, both platforms have their advantages and disadvantages. Consider your technical expertise, budget, and website goals when making your decision.

Imagine you're building a house. WordPress.com is like a pre-designed home kit, easy to assemble but limited in customization. WordPress.org is like a blank blueprint, allowing you to design and build your dream home from scratch, but requiring more effort and knowledge.

The beauty of WordPress is that it offers something for everyone, whether you're a tech-savvy professional or a complete novice. In the next chapter, we'll delve into the exciting world of setting up WordPress.org. You'll learn how to install WordPress, explore the dashboard, choose a theme, and start building your own website. Get ready to unleash your creativity and bring your online vision to life!

Comparing WordPress to Other Platforms

Alright, my dear, let's dive into the world of website platforms and see how WordPress stacks up against the competition. It's like comparing apples and oranges, but with a dash of digital spice!

First off, think about your website's purpose. Is it a personal blog where you share your love for knitting? Or maybe you're launching a small business selling handcrafted jewelry online? Depending on your goals, you'll find different platforms offer distinct advantages and disadvantages.

Website Builders: Easy Peasy, But Not Always the Best

Website builders, like Wix, Squarespace, and GoDaddy, are like pre-designed houses. They offer beautiful templates, drag-and-drop interfaces, and convenient tools to create a basic website without coding knowledge. It's like putting together a puzzle, but with a more sophisticated outcome.

These builders are perfect for folks who are just starting out and don't want to learn the complexities of WordPress. They're quick and easy to set up, and many offer mobile-friendly options. But, remember, you're limited to their pre-defined designs and features. It's like wearing a stylish outfit, but you can't customize the fabric or stitching.

WordPress: The Versatile Powerhouse

WordPress, on the other hand, is more like building a custom house. It's a flexible platform that gives you complete control over your website's design and functionality. It's a bit more complex, but you get a lot more creative freedom.

Think of WordPress like a blank canvas waiting for your artistic touch. You can create anything you imagine! Want to add a fancy online store to sell your wares? No problem! Need a forum for your community to connect? You got it! Want to integrate social media seamlessly? WordPress makes it happen.

The Battle of the Platforms: WordPress vs. the Rest

Now, let's compare WordPress with some other popular platforms, focusing on key features:

Customization: WordPress is the undisputed champion in this category. You have tons of options to tailor your website to your heart's content. From choosing themes to installing plugins, you can truly make your website unique. Website builders, on the other hand, offer limited customization possibilities. Think of it like choosing from a menu – you have choices, but they're pre-selected.

Flexibility: WordPress shines again when it comes to flexibility. You can create almost any type of website, from simple blogs to complex online stores. It's like a versatile tool that can handle any project. Website builders might struggle with more complex requirements, like creating a community forum or a membership site.

Cost: WordPress is surprisingly affordable. While website builders offer attractive pricing plans, many include hidden costs for advanced features. WordPress.org is free, but you'll need to pay for hosting and a domain name. However, with WordPress.com, you get both hosting and domain name included in their affordable plans.

Community: The WordPress community is vast and supportive. You'll find countless resources, tutorials, and forums where you can get help from experienced users. It's like having a network of friendly neighbors who are always ready to lend a hand.

Learning Curve: WordPress does have a steeper learning curve than website builders. You'll need to invest some time to understand the basics, but there are tons of resources to guide you along the way. Think of it like learning a new skill – the initial effort pays off in the long run.

WordPress.com vs. WordPress.org: Two Sides of the Same Coin

Let's clarify this often-confusing difference. WordPress.com and WordPress.org are both based on the same software, but they differ in how you use it:

WordPress.com: This is a hosted version of WordPress. They handle the technical aspects, such as hosting and updates, making it easier for beginners. It's like renting an apartment – you get a ready-to-go space with minimal responsibilities. However, you'll have less customization options compared to WordPress.org.

WordPress.org: This is the self-hosted version of WordPress. You'll need to find your own hosting provider and manage the technical details. It's like buying a house – you have complete control, but you're also responsible for the maintenance.

Choosing Your Perfect Platform: A Decision for Your Future Website

Ultimately, the best website platform for you depends on your specific needs, preferences, and budget. Website builders are a great option for beginners who want a quick and easy way to build a basic website. But, for maximum flexibility, customization, and control, WordPress is the clear winner.

Think of your website like a garden. If you want something low-maintenance and beautiful, website builders are perfect. But, if you're a passionate gardener who loves to experiment and create unique landscapes, then WordPress is your perfect companion.

With all this information, you're well on your way to making an informed decision about your website platform. Remember, my dear, this is just the beginning of your journey. We'll delve into the exciting world of WordPress in the next chapter, where you'll learn how to set up your own website and make it a masterpiece!

Understanding WordPresscom vs org

Now, let's talk about the two main flavors of WordPress: WordPress.com and WordPress.org. Imagine you're at a bakery: both offer you a delicious cake, but the ingredients and how you get them are different.

WordPress.com is like a pre-packaged cake from the bakery. You get a ready-made website with basic features, and you don't have to worry about the technical stuff like hosting or security. It's perfect for those who want a simple, straightforward way to create a website.

Pros of WordPress.com:
Easy Setup: Just sign up, choose a theme, and start adding your content. No technical knowledge required.
Free Plan Available: You can start with a free plan, which is great for testing the waters.
Built-in Security: WordPress.com takes care of website security and updates for you.
Beginner-Friendly: Ideal for those who are new to website building and want a simple solution.

Cons of WordPress.com:
Limited Customization: You have less control over the website's design and functionality compared to WordPress.org.
Fewer Features: Free plans have limited features and may require you to pay for upgrades.
Limited Plugin Options: You can't install all plugins, only those approved by WordPress.com.
Less Control Over Your Data: Your website is hosted on WordPress.com's servers, so you don't have full control over your data.

WordPress.org, on the other hand, is like a "make your own cake" option. You get all the ingredients—the core WordPress software, themes, and plugins—and you have complete freedom to create your dream website. You need to find a place to bake it (hosting), manage the ingredients (installation and updates), and decorate it according to your taste (customization).

Pros of WordPress.org:
Unlimited Customization: You have complete control over your website's design, functionality, and features.
Vast Plugin Library: Access to thousands of plugins that can add any feature imaginable to your website.
Full Control Over Your Data: You own your website and can host it wherever you choose.
Scalability: You can easily scale your website as your needs grow.

Cons of WordPress.org:
More Technical: You need to handle hosting, installation, updates, and security yourself.
Higher Initial Cost: You need to pay for hosting and a domain name, which can add up.
Steeper Learning Curve: Requires more technical knowledge and time to learn the ropes.

Choosing the Right Option

So, how do you know which WordPress is right for you? Here's a simple guide:

If you're a beginner looking for a simple, easy-to-use website without technical hassles, WordPress.com is a great option. It's like taking the "easy" route to baking.

If you're more experienced and want full control over your website's design, functionality, and features, WordPress.org is the way to go. It's like being the master baker, creating a cake exactly to your liking.

Let's break down each option with more detail.

WordPress.com: The Easy Bake Oven

Imagine a friendly bakery assistant guiding you through a pre-selected cake recipe. That's what WordPress.com is like—they hold your hand throughout the process, making it as simple as possible.

No Hosting Hassles: You don't need to worry about finding a web host or configuring server settings. WordPress.com handles all the technical back-end stuff.
Easy Installation: Just create an account and you're ready to go. There's no need to download or install software.
Beginner-Friendly Dashboard: The WordPress.com dashboard is designed with beginners in mind, making it easy to navigate and understand.
Pre-built Themes: A wide variety of free and paid themes are available to choose from. These themes are often designed with specific purposes in mind, like blogging, photography, or e-commerce.
Limited Plugins: While WordPress.com does have plugins, they are limited to those approved by the platform. This helps ensure a consistent experience for all users but may not always provide the specific features you need.
Built-in Security: WordPress.com takes care of security updates, making it easier to keep your website safe.
Free Plan: While limited in features, a free plan lets you get your feet wet and see if WordPress is right for you.

WordPress.org: The Master Baker's Delight

Think of WordPress.org as a well-stocked bakery with unlimited possibilities. You have access to all the ingredients, tools, and recipes to create your perfect masterpiece. But you're responsible for assembling everything and managing the baking process.

Complete Freedom: With WordPress.org, you have complete control over every aspect of your website. From the design to the functionality, you can customize it to your heart's content.
Unlimited Plugins: You can install any plugin you want from the vast WordPress plugin directory. This gives you access to an incredible range of features and capabilities for your website.
Full Hosting Control: You choose your web host and manage your server settings. This gives you greater flexibility and customization options.
Open-Source Platform: Because WordPress.org is open-source, you can access and modify the core software to your needs. This allows you to build unique and powerful websites.
Steeper Learning Curve: Getting started with WordPress.org requires more technical knowledge than WordPress.com. You need to understand concepts like hosting, domain names, and plugin installation.
Potential Security Issues: While WordPress.org is secure, you're responsible for managing security updates and implementing security measures.

Beyond the Cake Analogy

Think of your website as a house you're building. WordPress.com is like hiring a contractor to build a pre-designed home. It's easy and affordable, but you have limited control over the final design and features. WordPress.org, on the other hand, is like hiring an architect and building crew to construct a custom-designed home. It requires more planning and investment, but you have complete control over every aspect of the construction.

Ultimately, the best platform for you depends on your needs and preferences. If you're looking for a simple, easy-to-use website with minimal technical hassle, WordPress.com is the way to go. But if you're more experienced and want complete control over your website, WordPress.org is the perfect option.

A Word of Encouragement

Don't be intimidated by the technical aspects of website building. Whether you choose WordPress.com or WordPress.org, there are plenty of resources available to help you along the way.

Remember, you're not alone on this journey. There are countless online communities, tutorials, and support forums dedicated to helping WordPress users of all levels. And of course, this book is here to guide you every step of the way.

Now that you understand the key differences between WordPress.com and WordPress.org, you're ready to make an informed decision about which platform is right for you. In the next chapter, we'll dive into the exciting world of setting up your WordPress website!

Choosing the Right Platform for You

Now that we've explored the world of website builders and gotten acquainted with WordPress, it's time to make a decision: which platform is the right fit for you? This is a crucial step, as your choice will shape your entire website building journey. Let's break down the factors to consider when making this important decision.

Understanding Your Needs:

Before diving into the details of each platform, let's take a moment to reflect on your website's purpose and your own skill level.

What do you want your website to achieve? Are you aiming to create a simple online presence for your personal blog, a business website with e-commerce capabilities, or a complex portfolio showcase for your artistic work?
How much time and effort are you willing to invest? Website builders offer a more streamlined approach with less technical setup, while WordPress requires a bit more learning but offers greater flexibility and control.
What level of customization do you need? If you're comfortable with basic design adjustments, a website builder might suffice. However, if you envision a highly unique and personalized website, WordPress might be a better option.

Website Builders: The Quick and Easy Option

Website builders like Wix, Squarespace, GoDaddy, and Weebly have gained immense popularity due to their user-friendly interfaces and drag-and-drop functionalities. These platforms are designed to be accessible to anyone, even those with no prior technical experience.

The Pros:

Easy to Use: Website builders are known for their intuitive interfaces and drag-and-drop features, making it effortless to create visually appealing websites without any coding knowledge.
Fast Setup: You can have your website up and running within a few minutes, thanks to their streamlined setup process.
Mobile Optimization: Most website builders automatically optimize your website for mobile devices, ensuring a seamless experience for your visitors on smartphones and tablets.
Affordable Options: Website builders typically offer affordable plans, making them a budget-friendly option for individuals and small businesses.
Built-in Templates and Features: They come with a wide range of professionally designed templates and pre-built features, such as contact forms, image galleries, and even e-commerce capabilities, which can be customized to your liking.

The Cons:

Limited Customization: While website builders provide flexibility, their customization options are often limited compared to WordPress. You might find yourself restricted by pre-defined layouts and features.
Dependence on the Platform: You're entirely reliant on the website builder for hosting and updates. You don't have the same level of control as you would with WordPress.
Potential for Hidden Fees: Some website builders may have hidden fees for premium features or additional storage,

so it's essential to read the fine print before committing.
Lack of Flexibility: Website builders can be restrictive if you need advanced features or specific functionalities not offered by their pre-built options.

WordPress: The Powerhouse of the Web

WordPress has become the most popular website platform globally, powering millions of websites, from personal blogs to large businesses. It's known for its flexibility, powerful features, and vast community support.

The Pros:

Unlimited Customization: WordPress allows for complete control over your website's design, functionality, and content. You can modify every aspect of your site using themes, plugins, and custom coding if you're comfortable with it.
Open-Source and Free: WordPress is an open-source platform, meaning it's free to use and modify. You only need to pay for hosting and domain name registration.
Extensive Plugin Library: WordPress boasts a vast library of thousands of plugins that extend its functionality. You can easily add features such as e-commerce, SEO optimization, social media integration, and more.
Large Community Support: With a massive community of users and developers, you can find countless resources, tutorials, and support forums to help you with any WordPress-related queries.
Flexibility and Control: You have full control over your website's data and content. You can easily back up and migrate your website to another hosting provider if needed.

The Cons:

Learning Curve: WordPress requires a bit of a learning curve compared to website builders. You need to familiarize yourself with the platform, its interface, and basic coding concepts.
Technical Expertise Required: Depending on your website's complexity, you may need some technical skills to customize and manage WordPress.
Potentially More Expensive: While WordPress itself is free, you'll need to pay for hosting and domain name registration. You may also incur additional expenses for premium themes and plugins.
Security Responsibility: With greater control comes greater responsibility. You're responsible for keeping your WordPress site secure, which involves regular updates and security measures.

WordPress.com vs. WordPress.org: What's the Difference?

Often, beginners get confused by the distinction between WordPress.com and WordPress.org. While both platforms are based on WordPress, they offer different levels of control and features.

WordPress.com:

Hosted Platform: WordPress.com is a hosted platform, meaning they handle all the technical aspects of your website, including hosting, security, and updates.
Limited Customization: You have fewer customization options compared to WordPress.org. You're limited to pre-defined themes and features offered by WordPress.com.
Free Plan Available: WordPress.com offers a free plan with limited features, but you can upgrade to paid plans for more storage, customization, and advanced features.

WordPress.org:

Self-Hosted Platform: WordPress.org is a self-hosted platform. You need to find your own hosting provider and install WordPress on your server.
Full Customization: You have complete control over every aspect of your website, including themes, plugins, and code.
No Free Plan: WordPress.org doesn't offer a free plan, but it's free to download and use. You only need to pay for hosting and domain name registration.

Choosing the Right Path:

Choosing between website builders and WordPress is a personal decision. Consider the following factors to guide your choice:

Ease of Use: If you prioritize a seamless and user-friendly experience, website builders are a great option.
Customization: If you want complete control over your website's design and functionality, WordPress is the way to go.
Budget: Website builders offer affordable plans, while WordPress costs depend on your hosting provider and chosen theme and plugins.
Technical Skills: If you're comfortable with basic coding and technical setup, WordPress offers more flexibility.

Don't Be Afraid to Experiment:

Ultimately, the best way to decide is to try both options. Most website builders offer free trials, and you can download WordPress and experiment on your local computer before committing to a hosting provider.

Once you've explored both platforms and have a better understanding of their features and limitations, you'll be in a better position to make an informed decision that aligns with your website goals and your level of comfort with technology. Remember, there's no right or wrong answer; the ideal platform is the one that empowers you to create a website that you're proud of and that meets your unique needs.

Installing WordPress

Okay, you're ready to take the plunge and install WordPress! It's like getting the keys to your very own online house, and I'm here to guide you every step of the way. Don't worry if you've never done this before – I'll break it down into easy-to-follow steps, just like I would for my grandkids.

Now, remember how we talked about choosing a web hosting provider in Chapter 1? Well, you'll need to log into your hosting account to get started. Most hosting providers offer one-click WordPress installation, which makes the whole process a breeze. It's like having a handyman who comes in and sets up everything for you.

Let's take a look at a common scenario – let's say you've chosen a hosting provider like Bluehost. You'll typically find the WordPress installation option in your cPanel, which is like the control center for your hosting account. You can think of it as the back room where all the magic happens.

Here's how you'll typically find the WordPress installation option:

1. **Log into your Bluehost cPanel:** You'll usually find the login link in your email from Bluehost.
2. **Look for the "WordPress" or "Install WordPress" icon:** It's usually organized in a section like "Software/Services" or "Website Builders."
3. **Click on the icon:** This will launch the WordPress installation wizard.

Time for the Installation Wizard:

Once you've clicked on the installation icon, you'll be greeted by the wizard. It's a friendly guide that walks you through the process, just like a helpful neighbor.

1. **Choose a Domain Name:** It's important to decide which domain name you want to install WordPress on. If you have multiple domains, you can select from the list.
2. **Enter the Site Name:** This is what will appear at the top of your website. Feel free to get creative!
3. **Choose a Username and Password:** This is your gateway to managing your website, so keep these details safe and secure.
4. **Provide your Email Address:** This is how you'll receive important notifications and updates.
5. **Click on "Install Now" or "Install":** And that's it! The installation wizard will take care of the rest.

Waiting for the Magic to Happen:

Now comes the exciting part – the installation process will take a few minutes. Think of it as baking a cake – it needs a little time to rise and become delicious. You'll typically see a progress bar to keep you company.

Success! You're Now a WordPress Owner:

Once the installation is complete, you'll get a notification that your WordPress website is ready. You'll be given a link to your login page, usually something like "yourdomain.com/wp-admin."

Accessing Your WordPress Dashboard:

Now it's time to enter the heart of your website – the WordPress dashboard. This is where you'll spend most of your time, creating content, customizing your site, and managing everything.

1. **Go to the login page:** This is the link you were given after installation.
2. **Enter your username and password:** Remember the details you chose earlier.
3. **Click "Log In":** And welcome to your WordPress dashboard!

Exploring the Dashboard:

The WordPress dashboard is like a well-organized control panel, with different sections for each task.

Dashboard Overview: The dashboard gives you a quick snapshot of your website's activity, including recent posts, comments, and updates.
Posts: Here, you'll create and manage your website's content, whether it's blog posts, articles, or pages.
Media: This is where you upload and manage images, videos, and other media files.
Pages: Here you'll create static pages for your website, like an "About Us" or "Contact Us" page.
Comments: Here you'll see comments left by visitors and can approve or moderate them.
Appearance: This is where you can choose and customize your website's theme, change colors, and adjust fonts.
Plugins: This is where you can install additional tools and features to enhance your website's functionality.
Settings: This is where you'll find all the general settings for your website, including site name, language, and time zone.

Don't Be Afraid to Explore:

The WordPress dashboard may seem a little intimidating at first, but don't worry! It's designed to be user-friendly, and you can always explore different sections at your own pace.

A Little Extra Help:

If you find yourself needing a little extra guidance, WordPress has a helpful online documentation center. You can also search for tutorials on YouTube or look for resources from other WordPress enthusiasts.

Congratulations! You're Now a Website Builder:

You've taken the first exciting step in creating your website. Installing WordPress is like laying the foundation of your online home. Now you can get ready to start building, customizing, and bringing your website to life. In the next chapter, we'll dive into the world of themes and learn how to choose the perfect look for your website. Stay tuned!

Getting Familiar with the Dashboard

Now that you've successfully installed WordPress, it's time to dive into the heart of your website's control center: the dashboard. Think of it as your command center, where you'll manage every aspect of your website, from writing your first blog post to customizing your website's look and feel.

The WordPress dashboard is a user-friendly interface designed with beginners in mind. It's a central hub that brings together all the tools you need to build and maintain your website. When you log into your WordPress site, you'll be greeted by the dashboard, which is divided into various sections, each with its own set of features and tools. Let's take a tour and explore these sections:

The Top Bar

The first thing you'll notice is the top bar, which runs across the top of the screen. It's your quick access point to the most important areas of the dashboard. Let's break down what each section does:

1. **WordPress Logo:** Click on the WordPress logo in the top left corner to return to the dashboard's home screen. This is like your starting point, where you'll find quick access to recent activity and updates on your website.

2. **Site Title:** Next to the logo, you'll see your website's name. This is where you can change your website's title whenever you want, giving your website a new identity.

3. **Dashboard:** Clicking on the "Dashboard" link takes you back to the home screen of your dashboard. This is where you'll find a summary of your website's recent activity and important updates.

4. **Posts:** This section is where you'll create and manage all the content on your website. It's the heart of your website's storytelling. Think of it as your library of written content, where you'll write blog posts, create pages for your website, and manage everything from announcements to testimonials.

5. **Media:** Here you'll find all the images, videos, and other media files you upload to your website. It's your digital photo album, where you'll store all the visual elements that bring your website to life.

6. **Pages:** This is where you build the structural foundation of your website. Think of it as building a house, where you create the different rooms: About Us, Contact Us, and other static pages that tell your website's story.

7. **Comments:** This is where you'll manage the conversations happening on your website. It's your online forum, where you can respond to comments on your blog posts, engage with your audience, and build relationships with your visitors.

8. **Appearance:** This is where you unleash your creativity! Here you'll find all the tools you need to customize the look and feel of your website. It's your design studio, where you'll choose your website's theme, customize its colors, add widgets, and design the way your website looks and feels to your visitors.

9. **Plugins:** This is where you expand the power of your website. It's your toolkit, where you'll find tools that add extra functionality to your website, such as contact forms, social media integration, and much more.

10. **Users:** Here you'll manage the different users who have access to your website. It's your team management area, where you'll add new users, assign roles, and control who has access to what.

11. **Tools:** This is where you'll find various tools to help you manage your website, such as importing and exporting data, managing your website's files, and more.

12. **Settings:** This is where you'll configure the settings of your website, including general settings, writing settings, reading settings, discussion settings, media settings, and permalinks. It's your website's control panel, where you can tweak the underlying configuration and make sure everything works smoothly.

13. **Your Profile:** This is where you manage your own account and settings. It's your personal space on the website, where you can edit your profile information, change your password, and manage your account settings.

The Dashboard Home Screen

Let's go back to the dashboard's home screen. The home screen is your welcome center. It provides a quick overview of what's happening on your website. You'll see a summary of your recent activity, including the following:

1. **At a Glance:** This section gives you a quick summary of your website's status. Think of it as the dashboard of your car, where you can see key information like the number of posts you've published, the number of pages you've created, the number of comments you've received, and the number of users on your website.

2. **Activity:** This section shows you a timeline of recent events on your website. It's like your website's diary, where you can see what's been happening, including when you published a new post, when a new comment was submitted, and when someone registered as a new user.

3. **Quick Draft:** This is a handy little space where you can jot down quick notes or start a new post or page. It's your quick notepad, where you can capture ideas as they come to you.

4. **WordPress News:** This section keeps you updated on the latest news and updates from WordPress. It's like reading your favorite website building magazine, where you can stay informed about new features, security updates, and other important announcements.

Navigating the Dashboard

The WordPress dashboard is designed to be user-friendly and intuitive. You can navigate through it using the left sidebar, which contains a list of all the main sections of the dashboard. You can also use the search bar at the top of the dashboard to quickly find what you're looking for.

Understanding the Main Sections

Here's a closer look at each of the main sections of the dashboard:

1. **Posts:** This is where you create and manage all the content on your website. When you click on "Posts," you'll be taken to a page where you can view all your published posts, draft posts that you're working on, and create new posts. This is the heart of your website's storytelling, where you'll write engaging blog posts, create pages, and keep your visitors informed.

2. **Media:** This is where you'll find all the images, videos, and other media files you upload to your website. When you click on "Media," you'll be taken to a library of all your media files, where you can manage your digital assets. You can upload new media files, edit existing ones, and organize your files into folders.

3. **Pages:** Pages are static pages that make up the structural foundation of your website. They're the different "rooms" of your website, such as your "About Us" page, "Contact Us" page, and any other static pages you want to create. When you click on "Pages," you'll be taken to a list of all your pages, where you can create new pages, edit existing pages, and manage the structure of your website.

4. **Comments:** This is where you'll manage all the comments that people leave on your website. When you click on "Comments," you'll be taken to a list of all the comments that have been left on your website, where you can approve or reject comments, reply to comments, and manage the overall conversation on your website.

5. **Appearance:** This is where you'll customize the look and feel of your website. It's your design studio, where you can change the theme, colors, fonts, and other design elements of your website. When you click on "Appearance," you'll be taken to a list of all the options for customizing your website.

6. **Plugins:** This is where you'll add extra functionality to your website. It's your toolkit, where you'll find a library of plugins that can add features like contact forms, social media integration, SEO optimization, and more. When you click on "Plugins," you'll be taken to a list of all the plugins that are available for your website.

7. **Users:** This is where you'll manage the different users who have access to your website. It's your team management area, where you can add new users, assign roles, and control who has access to what. When you click on "Users," you'll be taken to a list of all the users on your website, where you can manage their roles, permissions, and access to your website.

8. **Tools:** This is where you'll find various tools to help you manage your website, such as importing and exporting data, managing your website's files, and more. When you click on "Tools," you'll be taken to a list of all the tools that are available to help you manage your website.

9. **Settings:** This is where you'll configure the settings of your website, including general settings, writing settings, reading settings, discussion settings, media settings, and permalinks. It's your website's control panel, where you can tweak the underlying configuration and make sure everything works smoothly. When you click on "Settings,"

you'll be taken to a list of all the settings that you can customize for your website.

Getting Familiar with the Dashboard

The best way to get familiar with the WordPress dashboard is to explore it and experiment with its features. Don't be afraid to click around and see what each section does. You can always undo any changes you make, and WordPress has a great help center that you can refer to if you have any questions.

Here are some tips for getting started:

1. **Start with the basics:** Explore the "Posts," "Pages," and "Media" sections first. These are the core sections where you'll be creating and managing most of the content on your website.
2. **Use the search bar:** If you can't find what you're looking for, use the search bar at the top of the dashboard. It can quickly help you find any page or section you need.
3. **Don't be afraid to experiment:** The WordPress dashboard is designed to be user-friendly, and it's easy to undo any changes you make. So, don't be afraid to experiment and see what each section does.
4. **Use the help center:** If you have any questions, you can always refer to the WordPress help center. It has a vast library of resources that can answer any questions you have about the dashboard.

As you become more comfortable with the WordPress dashboard, you'll be able to easily create and manage your website, add new features, and customize its appearance to your liking. The WordPress dashboard is your key to unlocking the power of WordPress, and with a little exploration, you'll be well on your way to building the website of your dreams.

Choosing a Theme

Now that you've set up your WordPress site, the next step is to give it a visual identity and personality: choosing a theme. Think of it as dressing up your website in a stylish outfit! Themes control the overall look and feel of your site, from the colors and fonts to the layout and structure.

You'll find a vast ocean of themes available, both free and premium. Choosing the right one is crucial, as it will influence how your visitors perceive your website. Think of your website's theme as its first impression, setting the tone for your content and your brand.

The Theme Jungle: Free vs. Premium

You've got two main paths in the theme jungle:

Free Themes: These are like the basic clothes you wear for a casual day out. They're readily available, often offering a decent look, and are a great starting point. Think of them as a free trial, where you can test out different styles without committing to a purchase. However, free themes might have fewer features and customization options than their premium counterparts.

Premium Themes: These are like the designer outfits you wear for a special occasion. They often come with advanced features, more styling flexibility, and professional support. They might require a one-time payment or a recurring subscription, but they can give your website a distinct and polished edge.

Factors to Consider When Choosing a Theme

Think about your website's purpose and the type of content you plan to share. Here are some crucial questions to ask yourself:

What's your website's niche? Is it a personal blog about your baking adventures, a business showcasing your services, or a portfolio showcasing your artistic creations?

What kind of style are you going for? Do you prefer a sleek and modern design, a classic and timeless look, or something fun and playful?

Who is your target audience? Consider their age, interests, and what kind of website experience they'd appreciate.

What features do you need? Do you need an online shop, a contact form, a newsletter signup, or a specific layout for your content?

Do you have the technical skills to customize a theme? Some themes are highly customizable, while others are more streamlined.

The Treasure Hunt for Your Perfect Theme

Now that you've considered these factors, it's time to explore the theme jungle. There are two main sources for finding themes:

The WordPress Theme Directory: Think of this as a massive online marketplace for free themes. It's a great place to start your search and browse through themes categorized by genre and features. You can preview them and check user reviews before making a decision.

Theme Marketplaces: These online marketplaces offer a curated selection of both free and premium themes. They often provide better quality control and offer more customization options, along with support and updates. Some popular theme marketplaces include:

ThemeForest: A massive marketplace with a vast selection of high-quality themes, both free and paid.
Elegant Themes: Known for its Divi theme, which is a highly customizable and versatile theme.
StudioPress: Specializes in Genesis Framework, a robust framework for building WordPress sites.

Diving into the Theme Details

Once you've found some promising themes, take a closer look at their features and details. Here are some things to check:

Responsiveness: Does the theme look good on all devices, like desktops, laptops, tablets, and smartphones? In this day and age, a responsive theme is essential for providing a seamless user experience.

Customization Options: Can you change colors, fonts, and layouts? How much control do you have over the theme's overall appearance?

Documentation: Is there a comprehensive guide on how to use and customize the theme? Good documentation can make your life much easier, especially if you're new to WordPress.

Updates: Are the theme developers actively updating the theme with new features and security fixes? Regular updates are crucial for ensuring compatibility and safety.

Customer Support: Do the theme developers offer support if you encounter issues? This can be especially helpful if you're not a tech whiz and need a helping hand.

Installing Your Chosen Theme

Once you've found a theme that suits your needs, it's time to install it. Here's how:

1. **Login to your WordPress Dashboard:** Access your website's administration panel by typing your website address followed by `/wp-admin/` in your browser.

2. **Navigate to Appearance > Themes:** Click on "Appearance" in the left sidebar, then select "Themes."

3. **Add New Theme:** Click on the "Add New" button at the top.

4. **Search or Upload:** You can either search for a theme in the WordPress theme directory or upload a premium theme you purchased from a marketplace.

5. **Install & Activate:** Once you've found the theme, click on "Install." After installation, click on "Activate" to make the theme live on your website.

Theme Customization: Making Your Website Unique

Now that your theme is installed, you can customize it to your liking. This is where the fun begins! WordPress makes it easy to change colors, fonts, and other elements, allowing you to create a website that truly reflects your brand and personality.

Theme Options: Many themes come with a built-in theme options panel, accessible through "Appearance > Customize" in your WordPress dashboard. Here you'll find various settings for changing the theme's colors, fonts, header, footer, and more.

Customizer: The WordPress Customizer is a powerful tool for real-time theme customization. You can preview changes live before saving them, ensuring that your edits are exactly what you envision.

Plugins: Plugins extend the functionality of WordPress, and there are many plugins specifically designed for theme customization. Some popular plugins for theme customization include:

Elementor: A drag-and-drop page builder that lets you create custom layouts and designs without coding.
Gutenberg: The latest WordPress block editor that offers a flexible and intuitive way to design your pages.
WP Customizer: This plugin adds additional customization options to the WordPress Customizer.

The Theme Journey: A Constant Evolution

Remember, your website's theme is not set in stone. As your website evolves, your content changes, and your brand grows, you might want to update your theme to reflect these changes. Don't be afraid to experiment and explore new themes!

The journey of choosing a theme is just one step in building your own website. You'll soon learn how to create engaging content, optimize your website for search engines, and build a vibrant online community. The best part? It's a journey you can embark on at your own pace, learning new things as you go.

Remember, I'm here to guide you every step of the way. Just like a patient granny, I'll be there to answer your questions, share my tips, and celebrate your successes.

Customizing Your Theme

Now, picture this: you've got your WordPress site all set up, and it's looking pretty good with your chosen theme. But you're not quite done yet! Just like you might personalize your home with a fresh coat of paint, new curtains, or rearranging the furniture, we can do the same for our website. This is where theme customization comes in, and it's the fun part where we can truly make our website our own.

Think of your theme as a beautiful canvas. It's already got the basic structure and design elements in place, but it's up to you to add those finishing touches that make it uniquely yours. Now, don't worry, you don't have to be a coding whiz to do this. WordPress offers a variety of user-friendly tools that let you customize your theme without writing a single line of code.

Let's imagine you're setting up a website to share your grandmother's amazing recipes. You choose a theme that has a clean, modern look with lots of white space, which is perfect for showcasing those delicious-looking photos. But, you want to add a personal touch. You might decide to change the color scheme to incorporate your grandmother's favorite hues, maybe a warm yellow and a comforting blue. You can also add a cute banner image with a welcoming message, perhaps something like "Grandma's Kitchen: Where Family Recipes Come Together."

But customization doesn't stop there! Maybe your theme has a sidebar with extra widgets. You can add a "Featured Recipes" widget to highlight your most popular dishes, or a "Contact Us" widget to make it easy for people to reach out and ask for more recipes. You can even personalize the fonts to match your grandmother's handwriting, making the site feel truly unique.

Now, you might be thinking, "How do I even start customizing this thing?" Don't worry, it's easier than you think! Most themes come with a built-in "Customizer" that you can access from your WordPress dashboard. The Customizer is like a visual playground where you can experiment with different settings without affecting your live website. You can tweak everything from colors and fonts to layout and widgets, and see how the changes look in real time.

If you're feeling adventurous, you might even want to dive into the theme's code using a code editor. But, don't worry, I'm here to guide you through that process as well. We'll cover everything from basic CSS customizations to adding custom code snippets.

Remember, the beauty of WordPress themes is that they are built with flexibility in mind. You have the power to adapt them to your specific needs and preferences. So, don't be afraid to experiment and have fun!

Here are some common areas where you might want to make theme customizations:

Colors and Fonts: One of the easiest ways to make your website feel like your own is by adjusting the colors and fonts. This is where the Customizer comes in handy. Many themes offer pre-defined color palettes, but you can also choose your own colors by using a color picker tool. Experiment with different combinations until you find a look that reflects your brand or personal style. When it comes to fonts, choose ones that are easy to read and complement your website's overall design.

Layout and Structure: Your theme's layout determines how content is arranged on each page. Some themes offer customizable layouts for different page types, such as home pages, blog posts, or product pages. The Customizer often provides options for changing the width of columns, adding sidebars, or adjusting the spacing between elements. You can also use widgets to add extra content elements, like image galleries or contact forms, to your sidebars or footers.

Header and Footer: The header is the top part of your website that usually contains your logo, navigation menu, and other important information. The footer is the bottom part that often includes copyright information, social media links, and additional content. The Customizer often allows you to upload your own logo, create custom menus, and add or remove elements from your header and footer.

Blog Posts and Pages: The layout and design of your blog posts and pages can also be customized to fit your content. You can adjust the size of featured images, the way comments are displayed, and the overall look and feel of your content sections.

Contact Form and Other Features: Many themes come with built-in contact forms, and you can customize these to collect the information you need from visitors. For example, you might want to add a field for visitors to provide their email address or include a message field for them to share their feedback. You can also add other features like social media sharing buttons, calendars, or search bars to enhance your website's functionality.

While the Customizer provides a lot of flexibility, sometimes you might need to go beyond its limits. This is where you can explore the theme's code. But, before you dive into the code, always make a backup of your website. It's like having a safety net in case anything goes wrong.

Here are some of the most common areas where you might want to make code customizations:

CSS (Cascading Style Sheets): CSS is the language that defines your website's visual appearance. You can use CSS to customize colors, fonts, spacing, and other design elements. If you're comfortable with CSS, you can make changes to your theme's stylesheet to fine-tune the look and feel of your website.

HTML (HyperText Markup Language): HTML is the language that structures your website's content. You can use HTML to add new elements to your pages, such as custom headings, paragraphs, images, or videos. If you know HTML, you can modify your theme's template files to customize the layout and content of your pages.

JavaScript (JS): JavaScript adds interactivity and functionality to your website. You can use JavaScript to create animations, forms, pop-ups, and other dynamic elements. If you have JavaScript skills, you can add custom scripts to your theme to enhance its functionality.

Don't worry if you're not a coding expert. There are tons of resources available to help you learn CSS, HTML, and JavaScript. You can find tutorials, online courses, and even free code generators that can help you create the code you need. Just remember to always test your code changes thoroughly before implementing them on your live website.

Now, let's get more specific about how to make some common customizations.

1. Changing Colors and Fonts:

Using the Customizer: Most themes provide an easy way to change colors and fonts through the Customizer. Look for options like "Colors" or "Typography" in the Customizer menu. You can choose from pre-defined color palettes or use a color picker to create your own custom colors. You can also select from different font families, adjust font sizes, and change line heights.

Editing the Theme's Stylesheet: If you want more control over your colors and fonts, you can edit the theme's stylesheet. The stylesheet is a CSS file that defines your website's visual style. To edit the stylesheet, you'll need to access your theme's files through your WordPress dashboard's Appearance -> Theme Editor.

2. Adding a Sidebar:

Using the Customizer: Some themes have a built-in option to add or remove sidebars from your pages. Check for a "Sidebar" section in your Customizer's "Layout" settings.

Using Widgets: Even if your theme doesn't have a built-in sidebar option, you can still add one using widgets. Widgets are small, reusable content elements that can be placed in different areas of your website, including sidebars.

3. Creating a Custom Menu:

Using the WordPress Menu System: WordPress provides an easy-to-use menu system that allows you to create custom menus for your website. Go to Appearance -> Menus in your

WordPress dashboard. You can add new menu items, arrange them in the order you want, and assign them to different menu locations on your website.

Editing the Theme's Template Files: If you want to customize the way your menus are displayed, you can edit your theme's template files. The template files are the files that determine how content is displayed on your website.

4. Adding Social Media Links:

Using Widgets: Many themes have widgets that allow you to add social media links to your sidebar, footer, or other areas of your website.

Using Plugins: You can also use plugins to add social media sharing buttons to your blog posts and pages. Plugins are small pieces of code that add additional features to your website. There are many plugins available that can easily add social media sharing buttons to your website.

5. Creating a Custom Contact Form:

Using Built-in Form Tools: Many themes have built-in form tools that make it easy to create a contact form. You can typically customize the form's fields, such as name, email address, and message, to collect the information you need from visitors.

Using Plugins: There are several plugins available that allow you to create custom contact forms with more advanced features, such as spam protection, email notifications, and integration with other services.

6. Adding Custom Code Snippets:

Using the "Theme Editor": If you want to add custom CSS, HTML, or JavaScript code to your website, you can do it through the "Theme Editor" in your WordPress dashboard. Be sure to make a backup of your theme before making any changes.

Using Plugins: There are also plugins that allow you to insert custom code snippets into your website without editing your theme files. These plugins provide a more secure and convenient way to add custom code to your website.

Theme customization is a fun and rewarding part of building a website. It's a great way to make your website truly your own and enhance its look, feel, and functionality. Just remember to experiment, have fun, and always back up your website before making any changes.

Essential Plugins to Install

Now that you've chosen your WordPress theme and have a beautiful, functional website structure, let's delve into the world of plugins! Plugins are like little helpers that add extra functionality to your website. Think of them as apps for your website, allowing you to do things like add contact forms, manage your social media presence, or even sell products online.

Just like with any software, plugins can either make your life easier or create a frustrating mess. It's crucial to be selective about which plugins you choose, as too many can slow down your website or even cause compatibility issues.

I'll share some of my favorite, tried-and-true plugins that will help you create a fantastic website. We'll cover essential plugins that are must-haves for functionality and security, and then we'll explore some advanced plugins that might be helpful depending on your website's specific needs.

The Must-Have Plugins: Your Website's Swiss Army Knife

Let's start with the essential plugins that every WordPress website should have. These are like the basic tools in your website toolbox, helping you manage content, improve security, and ensure your site is running smoothly.

1. Contact Form 7: For Easy Communication

Imagine this: you've created a beautiful website showcasing your photography, but there's no way for potential clients to reach you. A contact form plugin like Contact Form 7 solves this problem! This plugin allows you to easily add contact forms to any page on your website, enabling visitors to send you messages without needing to disclose their email addresses.

Think of a contact form as a virtual receptionist. It's a professional way to handle inquiries and keeps your personal email address private. It's simple to use and customize, allowing you to create forms with different fields, such as name, email, message, and even dropdown menus for specific inquiries.

2. Yoast SEO: Mastering Search Engine Optimization

You've poured your heart and soul into creating amazing content for your website, but how will people find it? That's where Yoast SEO comes in. This plugin is a game-changer for anyone who wants to improve their website's visibility in search engines like Google.

Imagine Yoast SEO as your website's personal SEO coach. It analyzes your content and provides suggestions for improvement, ensuring your website is optimized for search engines. This plugin helps you create keyword-rich titles and descriptions, optimize your images, and even check your website's readability.

Don't let your website get lost in the vast sea of internet content. Yoast SEO can help you stand out and reach a wider audience.

3. Akismet: Protecting Your Website from Spam

We've all seen spam comments lurking on websites. It's annoying and can make your website look unprofessional. Akismet, a free plugin developed by Automattic, the company behind WordPress.com, is your spam-fighting superhero.

Imagine Akismet as a watchful guardian, filtering out spam comments before they even reach your website. It uses a powerful algorithm to detect and block spam, keeping your comment sections clean and focused on genuine feedback.

4. WP Super Cache: Speeding Up Your Website

Remember that slow website we discussed earlier? A caching plugin like WP Super Cache is the solution. It creates static HTML versions of your website's pages, allowing them to load much faster for visitors.

Think of WP Super Cache as your website's speed demon. It pre-loads your website's pages so they're ready to be served instantly to visitors, making your website snappier and providing a better user experience.

5. UpdraftPlus: Safeguarding Your Website's Data

We've all heard horror stories about websites getting hacked or losing valuable data. Don't let this happen to you! UpdraftPlus is a powerful backup plugin that creates regular backups of your entire WordPress website, including your themes, plugins, and database.

Think of UpdraftPlus as your website's trusty backup plan. It regularly saves copies of your website's data, ensuring you can easily restore everything if something unexpected happens. This plugin can also be used to easily migrate your website from one hosting account to another.

Beyond the Basics: Advanced Plugins for Enhanced Functionality

Now that we've covered the must-have plugins, let's explore some advanced plugins that can add exciting features to your website, depending on your specific needs.

1. WooCommerce: Turning Your Website into an Online Store

Do you have a passion for crafting beautiful jewelry or selling vintage clothing? WooCommerce is your go-to plugin for turning your website into a fully functional online store. It seamlessly integrates with WordPress, allowing you to easily manage your products, inventory, orders, and even handle payments.

Think of WooCommerce as your website's digital storefront. It provides everything you need to create a professional online shop, from product displays and shopping carts to secure payment gateways and shipping options.

2. Elementor: Drag-and-Drop Website Building

Have you ever dreamt of creating a stunning website without needing to write code? Elementor, a popular page builder plugin, allows you to design beautiful and functional websites using a simple drag-and-drop interface. It's a visual website builder that lets you create custom layouts, add widgets, and even design dynamic content.

Think of Elementor as your website's visual editor. It empowers you to create a website that truly reflects your vision, without needing to learn complex coding.

3. Jetpack: Adding Power to Your Website

Jetpack is a versatile plugin from Automattic, offering a wide range of features that can enhance your website's performance, security, and overall functionality. It includes features like site analytics, spam protection, social media sharing, and even a contact form builder.

Think of Jetpack as your website's multi-tool. It brings together a variety of useful features to streamline your website management.

Choosing Plugins: A Few Tips for Success

With so many plugins available, it can be overwhelming to choose the right ones. Here are a few tips to help you make wise decisions:

Start with the essentials: Focus on installing the must-have plugins we discussed earlier.
Consider your website's needs: Think about the specific features you need for your website, such as contact forms, e-commerce, or social media integration.
Read reviews: Before installing a plugin, take the time to read reviews from other WordPress users to get a sense of its functionality and reliability.
Prioritize security: Always prioritize security by choosing reputable plugins from trusted developers.
Keep it simple: Avoid installing too many plugins, as this can slow down your website's performance.

Remember, plugins are like ingredients in a delicious recipe. Choosing the right ones can make your website a masterpiece. Happy website building!

Writing Compelling Blog Posts

Okay, let's dive into the captivating world of blog posts! Think of your blog as a cozy coffee shop where you share your thoughts, experiences, and expertise with the world. You want to make sure your visitors feel welcome, intrigued, and eager to sip on your words.

Crafting Enchanting Blog Posts

Now, writing compelling blog posts is all about connecting with your readers on a personal level. Remember, you're not just throwing words onto a page; you're weaving a story, sharing insights, and sparking conversations.

First Impressions Count

Hook 'em from the Start: Just like a good mystery novel, you need to grab your reader's attention right away. A compelling headline is crucial. Think of it like a catchy song title – it needs to make people want to click! Here are some ideas:

Ask a Question: "Is Your Website Missing These Essential Elements?" This piques their curiosity and makes them want to find out the answer.

Promise Value: "Learn the Secret to Building a Website That Converts" This implies they'll gain something valuable from reading your post.

Use Strong Verbs: "Unlock the Power of Social Media for Your Business" This makes your post sound dynamic and action-oriented.

Tell a Story: Everyone loves a good story! Think of your blog post as a chance to share an anecdote, a personal experience, or a case study that showcases your expertise.

Let your readers get to know you and see how you apply your knowledge in the real world.

Start with a personal anecdote: "Remember that time you struggled to find a specific recipe online? I felt that frustration too, and it inspired me to create this website..." This connects with readers on a human level.

Share a case study: "A local bakery was struggling to reach new customers. I helped them create a user-friendly website and within three months, their sales increased by 20%! This demonstrates your expertise and helps readers see the potential impact.

Keep it Conversational: Imagine you're chatting with a friend over coffee. Use a relaxed and friendly tone. Avoid jargon and technical terms that your audience might not understand.

Building Your Content

Structure Matters: Just like a well-organized home, your blog posts need a clear structure to guide your readers. Use bullet points, numbered lists, and subheadings to break up the text and make it easier to digest.

Subheadings: Use subheadings to create natural breaks and make your post more visually appealing. Each subheading should signal a new idea or section of your post.

Bullet Points & Lists: These are perfect for summarizing key points, outlining steps, or presenting a series of ideas. They make your content more concise and visually engaging.

Add Images & Videos: Pictures speak a thousand words! Don't just rely on text. Include relevant images, videos, and infographics to break up the monotony and add visual interest.

Think about your visuals: Choose images that are high-quality and relevant to your topic.

Use video strategically: Videos can be a great way to explain complex concepts or showcase your personality.
Don't Forget SEO: SEO (Search Engine Optimization) helps your website get found by people searching online. It's like putting up a "Welcome" sign for your website so search engines can understand what your content is about.
Keywords: Research and use relevant keywords throughout your post.
Meta Descriptions: Write concise and compelling meta descriptions that will encourage people to click on your blog post in search results.

Cultivating Engagement

Ask Questions: Encourage interaction by asking questions at the end of your post or throughout the content.
Open-ended questions: "What are your favorite resources for learning about website building?" These prompt thoughtful responses.
Poll questions: "Do you prefer using a website builder or WordPress?" These create a sense of community.
Promote Your Post: Share your blog post on social media, email it to your subscribers, and engage with comments.
Use relevant hashtags: These help people discover your post on social media.
Respond to comments: Show your readers that you value their input and want to create a dialogue.

The Power of Consistency

Create a Content Calendar: This is a schedule that outlines your blog posting frequency and topics. Consistency helps you build a loyal audience.
Set realistic goals: Start with a manageable posting schedule, such as once a week or once a month.

Plan your topics: Brainstorm ideas ahead of time, and you'll never be stuck for what to write.

Remember: Your blog is your platform to connect with your audience, share your passion, and build a community. Have fun, be authentic, and let your personality shine through!

Adding Images and Media

Let's dive into the world of images and media! Just like adding a sprinkle of sugar to your favorite dessert, images and media can make your blog posts come alive and capture your readers' attention.

Think of it this way: you're telling a story about your latest baking adventure. You could just describe how you kneaded the dough, how it rose beautifully, and how you carefully placed it in the oven. But wouldn't it be much more captivating if you showed a picture of the golden-brown bread coming out of the oven, or a short video of you mixing the dough?

Images and media aren't just about making things look pretty; they can really boost your blog posts' engagement and make them more shareable. They're like the spice that adds extra flavor and dimension to your storytelling.

Why Use Images and Media?

Here's a glimpse into how images and media can work their magic:

Capture Attention: In the vast sea of online content, a well-placed image can quickly grab attention. It acts like a visual headline, drawing readers in and making them want to explore further.
Visual Storytelling: Images and videos can convey emotions and experiences much more powerfully than words alone. They allow your readers to feel the joy of your baking success or the warmth of your grandma's kitchen.

Break Up Text: Imagine reading a long block of text without any visual breaks. It can be overwhelming! Images and media act as visual "breathers," making your blog posts more digestible and easier to read.
Boost Engagement: Images and media encourage readers to interact with your content. They're more likely to like, comment, share, and even leave a positive review on your blog post.
SEO Benefits: Search engines love images and videos! They help your blog posts rank higher in search results, increasing your website's visibility and bringing in more visitors.

Choosing the Right Images and Media

Now that you understand the power of images and media, let's talk about choosing the right ones for your blog posts:

High-Quality Images: Aim for images that are sharp, clear, and visually appealing. If you're not a professional photographer, there are plenty of free and paid stock photo websites where you can find stunning images to use. Just make sure to check the licensing terms before using any images!
Relevance to Content: Your images and media should be directly related to your blog post. Don't just randomly throw in an image for the sake of it. Make sure it adds value to your content and enhances your storytelling.
File Size Matters: Images can take up a lot of space, which can slow down your website's loading time. Optimize your images by compressing them without sacrificing quality. Aim for a balance between image quality and file size.
Video Power: Videos can be a great way to add a personal touch and show your audience what you're really like. You can create short videos about your baking adventures, share tips and tricks, or even do a product review.

Copyright Considerations: Remember to always respect copyright laws. If you're using images or videos from other sources, make sure you have the right to use them. You can check for Creative Commons licenses or purchase royalty-free images and videos.

Where to Find Images and Media

Finding high-quality images and media for your blog posts is easier than you might think. Here are a few reliable sources:

Free Stock Photo Websites: Websites like Unsplash, Pexels, Pixabay, and Flickr offer a vast collection of free high-resolution images. You can often find images that are free to use for commercial purposes as well.

Paid Stock Photo Websites: If you need a more specialized collection or high-quality images for commercial use, you can consider subscribing to paid stock photo websites like Shutterstock, Adobe Stock, and iStockphoto.

Create Your Own: If you have a good camera and some basic photo editing skills, you can create your own images. This is a great way to add a personal touch and ensure your images are unique.

Your Own Collection: Don't forget to leverage your own collection of photos and videos. If you've captured some amazing images while baking or traveling, use them on your blog!

Adding Images and Media to Your WordPress Posts

WordPress makes it incredibly easy to add images and media to your blog posts. Just follow these simple steps:

1. **Write Your Blog Post:** Start by writing your blog post as usual, just like you would write a story.

2. **Add an Image or Media:** When you reach the point where you want to insert an image or video, click on the "Add Media" button in the toolbar above your post's editor.
3. **Choose Your Image or Media:** You'll be presented with a pop-up window where you can upload an image or video from your computer or browse the media library.
4. **Upload Your Image or Video:** Select the image or video you want to use and click on the "Upload" button.
5. **Adjust Image Settings:** Once your image is uploaded, you can adjust its size, alignment, and caption.
6. **Insert Media:** Click on the "Insert into post" button to place the image or video in your blog post.

Tips for Using Images and Media Effectively

Here are some tips to help you make the most of images and media in your blog posts:

Use a Consistent Image Style: Maintain a visual theme throughout your blog posts. Use similar image styles, color palettes, and sizes to create a cohesive and professional look.
Optimize Image Alt Text: Alt text is an important accessibility feature that describes the image to screen readers and search engines. Use relevant keywords in your alt text to improve your blog post's SEO.
Pay Attention to File Sizes: Make sure your images and media are optimized for fast loading times. Use a tool like TinyPNG or Compressor.io to compress your images without sacrificing quality.
Don't Overdo It: Avoid overwhelming your readers with too many images or media files. Keep it balanced and ensure your images and media complement your blog posts.

Let's Get Creative!

Remember, the key is to have fun and experiment with images and media. Use them to tell your story, engage your audience, and make your blog posts stand out. Just like grandma adds a dash of spice to her dishes, you can add a dash of visual magic to your blog posts with images and media. Your blog will thank you for it!

Understanding SEO Basics

Okay, let's dive into the world of SEO, a key ingredient for making your website a tasty treat for search engines.

Imagine you're baking a delicious cake. You want everyone to savor its flavors, right? That's exactly what SEO does for your website. It's like adding the perfect pinch of spices and the right amount of sugar to make your website irresistible to search engines like Google, Bing, and Yahoo.

So, what exactly is SEO? It stands for **Search Engine Optimization** , and it's the art and science of making your website more visible in search results. Think of it like a recipe for online success. Just like a recipe has ingredients and steps, SEO has techniques and strategies that help your website stand out from the crowd.

When someone searches for something online, whether it's a recipe for apple pie or information about a new smartphone, search engines work hard to show the most relevant and helpful results. And that's where SEO comes into play.

Here's a breakdown of some SEO basics that will help your website get noticed:

Keywords: The Spice Rack of SEO

Keywords are the words and phrases people type into search engines to find information. They are like the spices you add to your cake to bring out unique flavors.

Think like a searcher: When you're crafting your website content, put yourself in the shoes of someone searching for

information. What would they type into Google to find what you offer?
Example: If you're running a bakery, you might use keywords like "bakery near me," "best cupcakes," or "custom cake orders."
Research is key: There are tools available to help you find popular keywords related to your website. You can use online keyword research tools or even simply browse through Google's autocomplete suggestions when you start typing in the search bar.

Content is King: The Cake Batter

Just like cake batter forms the base of your delicious creation, content is the foundation of your website.

High-quality content: It's all about creating engaging, informative, and valuable content for your audience. Think about it as sharing your passion and knowledge with the world.
Example: If you have a website about gardening, you might write articles about how to start a vegetable garden, tips for growing flowers, or recipes using fresh herbs.
Regular updates: Keep your website content fresh and interesting. Regularly adding new blog posts, articles, or other types of content will not only keep your audience engaged but also signal to search engines that your site is active and relevant.

Backlinks: The Icing on the Cake

Backlinks are like the icing on your cake – they add an extra layer of sweetness and attractiveness.

What are backlinks? They are links from other websites to your website. Search engines see these as a vote of

confidence in your website's credibility and relevance.
Example: If your gardening website gets a link from a well-established gardening magazine or website, it's like getting a stamp of approval from an expert.
How to get backlinks: You can try to get backlinks by guest blogging on other websites, participating in online forums, or creating content that others would find valuable and link to.

Technical SEO: The Baking Equipment

Technical SEO is like having the right tools and equipment in your kitchen. It ensures that your website is built and structured in a way that search engines can easily understand and crawl.

Mobile-friendly design: In today's mobile-first world, it's crucial that your website is designed to be user-friendly on both desktops and mobile devices.
Fast loading speed: Search engines favor websites that load quickly. Slow-loading websites can deter visitors and hurt your SEO ranking.
Website security: It's important to ensure that your website is secure, using HTTPS to protect sensitive information.

Understanding SEO is a Journey

Remember, SEO is a long-term strategy. It takes time, effort, and consistent work to see results. Think of it as a marathon, not a sprint. The more you learn and apply SEO principles, the more your website will flourish.

A Granny's Wisdom for Website Success

Don't be afraid to learn: The world of SEO can seem complicated, but it's just like learning a new recipe – you

start with the basics and gradually build your knowledge.
Consistency is key: Just like baking a cake, you need to be consistent in your efforts to achieve the best results. Keep updating your content, optimizing for keywords, and building backlinks to see your website grow.
Never stop experimenting: There are always new SEO techniques and strategies emerging. Don't be afraid to try new things and see what works best for your website.

With a little bit of patience, effort, and a sprinkle of SEO magic, your website will soon be a delicious treat that everyone will want to savor!

Creating a Content Calendar

Now that you have your content ready, it's time to organize it and put it on a schedule with a content calendar. A content calendar is like a roadmap for your website. It helps you keep track of what you plan to post, when, and why. It's an essential tool for keeping your website fresh, engaging, and consistent.

Think of it like a calendar you use to plan your personal life. You wouldn't just randomly show up at events without any preparation, right? The same goes for your website. A well-planned content calendar ensures you're always ready to share something interesting with your visitors.

Let's dive into the benefits of a content calendar:

Staying Consistent and Organized: Imagine you're reading a blog, and you find a post about baking delicious cookies. You enjoy it, but you have no idea when the next post will be. You might lose interest and forget about the blog altogether. But with a content calendar, you know exactly when to expect the next recipe, keeping you engaged and coming back for more.

Prepping Ahead: A content calendar helps you plan your content in advance. You can draft your posts, gather your images, and schedule them for release in advance. This saves you time and stress, ensuring you don't have to scramble at the last minute to create content.

Reaching the Right Audience at the Right Time: Have you ever wondered when the best time to post on social media is? Well, a content calendar can help you figure that out. You can analyze your audience's behavior and schedule your posts during the times they're most active.

Tracking Progress and Measuring Success: A content calendar is not just about planning; it's also a tool for measuring your progress. You can track your website's performance by analyzing the success of your content. Did a certain post receive a lot of likes or shares? You can then identify your most successful content and create more of it.

Planning Your Content:

Now that you understand the benefits of a content calendar, let's talk about how to create one. There are many online tools and software available, but you can start with a simple spreadsheet or a calendar app.

Here's a simple structure for your content calendar:

1. **Date:** This column lists the date you plan to publish your content.
2. **Post Title:** Give each post a clear and concise title.
3. **Content Type:** Is it a blog post, a video, an infographic, or something else?
4. **Topic:** What will your post be about?
5. **Keywords:** What keywords will help people find your content online?
6. **Links:** If you're linking to other resources, list them here.
7. **Social Media:** Plan when and how you'll share your content on social media.
8. **Call to Action:** What do you want your readers to do after reading your content? Do you want them to sign up for a newsletter, purchase a product, or leave a comment?

Filling Your Content Calendar:

Think about the topics you want to cover. You can create a content calendar for an entire year or just for a few months. Start by brainstorming. What are your website's goals? Who is your target audience? What are they interested in?

Here are some ideas to get you started:

Seasonal Content: You can create content based on holidays, seasons, or special events. For example, in the summer, you might write about summer recipes, travel tips, or gardening tips.
Trending Topics: Research what's popular in your niche or industry. Write about trending topics that your audience is interested in.
Behind-the-Scenes Content: Offer a glimpse into your business or personal life. Share your experiences, challenges, and successes.
Tips and Tutorials: Provide valuable information that helps your audience learn and solve problems.
Q&A: Answer frequently asked questions about your niche or industry.

Remember:

Be consistent. Try to post regularly.
Don't be afraid to experiment. Test different types of content and see what performs best.
Track your results. Use your calendar to analyze your website's performance and make adjustments as needed.

Example Content Calendar:

Let's say you have a website about travel. Here's a sample content calendar for a month:

Week 1:

Monday: "Top 10 Places to Visit in Italy" – Blog post with stunning visuals
Wednesday: "Packing Hacks for Your Next Trip" – Infographic
Friday: "Best Travel Apps for Budget Travelers" – Video

Week 2:

Monday: "How to Plan a Romantic Getaway" – Blog post with tips and advice
Wednesday: "Backpacking Essentials for Adventure Seekers" – List post
Friday: "Travel Photography Tips for Beginners" – Video with easy-to-follow instructions

Week 3:

Monday: "My Experience Hiking the Inca Trail" – Personal experience blog post
Wednesday: "How to Find Cheap Flights" – Blog post with helpful links and strategies
Friday: "Top 5 Destinations for Solo Travelers" – List post with photos and descriptions

Week 4:

Monday: "The Ultimate Guide to Traveling with Kids" – Comprehensive blog post
Wednesday: "Travel Insurance: What You Need to Know" – Informative blog post
Friday: "How to Stay Safe While Traveling Abroad" – Tips and safety advice

This example showcases different content types, relevant topics, and a plan for consistent posting throughout the month. Remember to personalize this framework according to your specific website, niche, and audience.

A content calendar is an investment in your website's success. It helps you stay organized, reach the right audience, and track your progress. It's a tool that every website owner should use. So, get started today and create a content calendar that helps you achieve your online goals!

Engaging with Your Audience

Now that you've got some amazing content up on your website, it's time to start interacting with your audience! It's like hosting a party, and the more you engage with your guests, the better the time everyone has. Think of your website visitors as curious friends who are interested in what you have to say.

First, let's talk about **comments** . They're a fantastic way to get your readers talking and sharing their thoughts on your posts. Imagine a cozy living room where everyone feels comfortable sharing their ideas, just like in a good old-fashioned coffee klatch.

Encourage comments: Make it clear that you're happy to hear from your visitors. Put a friendly invitation at the end of each post, like "Let me know what you think in the comments below!"
Respond to comments: Take the time to reply to each comment, even if it's just a simple "Thank you for sharing your thoughts!" It shows that you care and are listening.
Ask questions: Don't just leave it up to your readers to comment. Pose some thought-provoking questions to get them thinking and sharing their own experiences.
Keep the conversation going: Once you've received a few comments, don't let the conversation fizzle out. Reply with additional insights, ask further questions, and keep the dialogue lively.

Think of your website as a place where you can build a community of people who share similar interests. And one of the best ways to foster that community is through **social media** .

Choose the right platforms: Not every social media platform is right for every website. Consider your target audience and where they are most active. If you're a knitter sharing your craft, you'll probably find more engagement on Pinterest and Instagram than on LinkedIn.
Share your content: Don't be shy! Promote your latest blog posts, videos, or images on your social media accounts to get more eyeballs on your content. Think of it as spreading the word about your website's grand opening.
Interact with your followers: Social media is all about being social! Respond to comments, share relevant articles or posts from others, and join conversations on topics related to your niche.
Use relevant hashtags: Hashtags are like breadcrumbs that lead people to your content. Use them to categorize your posts and make it easier for people to find you when they're searching for information. Think of them as a way to connect with those who share similar interests.

Remember, the key to engaging with your audience is to be authentic, genuine, and helpful. Treat your readers like you would treat a good friend. Be patient and understanding, and don't be afraid to share your own experiences and knowledge. The more you connect with your audience, the more rewarding your website building journey will be.

Now, let's talk about a really important ingredient for engaging with your audience: **stories** . Stories have a way of connecting with people on a deep level. They make your content more memorable, relatable, and impactful.

Share personal stories: Don't be afraid to open up and share your own experiences. What challenges have you faced? What lessons have you learned? What successes have you celebrated? Your personal stories can help your readers feel

like they know you and connect with you on a personal level.
Tell customer stories: If you're running a business, you can share stories about satisfied customers. How did your products or services help them? What impact did they have on their lives? Customer stories are powerful testimonials that can build trust and credibility.
Use storytelling techniques: There are many different storytelling techniques you can use to make your content more engaging. For example, you can use vivid descriptions, dialogue, and suspense to keep your readers hooked.
Keep your stories concise and to the point: Nobody wants to read a novel-length story on your website. Focus on telling a compelling story that makes a point or delivers a message.

Stories are a powerful tool for engaging with your audience and creating a lasting impression. Use them wisely and you'll be well on your way to building a thriving online community.

Let's talk about another important aspect of engaging with your audience: **creating a sense of community** . Your website is more than just a collection of content—it's a place where people can come together, connect, and share their thoughts.

Host contests and giveaways: Contests and giveaways are a great way to generate excitement and reward your loyal followers. You can give away products, services, or even gift cards. Be sure to promote the contest on your social media channels to reach a wider audience.
Start a forum or discussion board: A forum or discussion board is a great place for your visitors to ask questions, share their experiences, and connect with each other. It's like

having a virtual coffee klatch where everyone can chat about their shared interests.

Encourage feedback and suggestions: Don't just assume you know what your audience wants. Ask for their feedback and suggestions. What do they like about your website? What could be improved? Their input will help you make your website even better.

Recognize and celebrate your followers: Show appreciation for your loyal followers by giving them a shout-out, featuring their content, or awarding them special recognition. It's like giving them a virtual pat on the back for being such great supporters.

Building a strong sense of community is an essential part of engaging with your audience. It's about creating a space where people feel welcome, valued, and connected.

Now let's talk about **SEO** , which stands for Search Engine Optimization. It's like making your website more visible to people who are searching for information online. Think of it as making your website's front porch more inviting so people can easily find their way in.

Use relevant keywords: Keywords are the words and phrases that people type into search engines when they're looking for information. When you use relevant keywords in your content, you're making it easier for search engines to find and display your website in search results.

Optimize your page titles and descriptions: Your page titles and descriptions are the first things people see when they're searching for information on a search engine. Make sure they're compelling and accurately reflect the content of your pages.

Create high-quality content: Search engines love high-quality content that's informative, engaging, and relevant.

Write blog posts, create videos, and share images that people will actually want to read, watch, and share.

Build backlinks: Backlinks are links from other websites to your website. They're like endorsements from other people who think your website is valuable. The more backlinks you have, the higher your website will rank in search results.

SEO is a continuous process, not a one-time fix. It takes time and effort to build a strong SEO strategy, but it's worth it. The more people who can find your website, the more potential you have to reach your audience and build a thriving online presence.

Finally, let's talk about a crucial element of engaging with your audience: **being consistent** . Consistency is key to building a loyal following. Think of it like tending to a garden—you have to nurture your audience with regular content and interaction to keep them coming back for more.

Establish a posting schedule: Decide how often you'll post new content and stick to that schedule as much as possible. Whether it's once a week, twice a month, or even daily, consistency helps your readers know when to expect new content and keeps them engaged.

Respond to comments and messages promptly: Don't let your readers feel like they're talking to a ghost. Respond to comments and messages as soon as you can, even if it's just a quick acknowledgement that you've received their message.

Be active on social media: Regularly share your website's content on social media, interact with your followers, and join conversations about your niche. Consistency helps you stay top of mind and build stronger connections with your audience.

Remember, building an audience takes time and effort. But by being consistent, authentic, and engaging, you can build a loyal following that will support your website's growth and success.

Exploring Advanced Plugins

Now that you've got your website looking spiffy with a great theme and some essential plugins, it's time to dive into the world of **advanced plugins**. These are like the power tools of your website, giving you extra abilities that can really boost its functionality and impact.

Think of it like adding those cool features to your car, like a GPS navigation system, a powerful sound system, or maybe even a back-up camera! Advanced plugins can do all sorts of things to make your website more engaging, interactive, and efficient.

Opening Up a World of Possibilities

Imagine you're baking a delicious cake. The basic ingredients, like flour, sugar, and eggs, are like your website's core elements. But those extra ingredients, like spices, nuts, and special flavorings, are like the advanced plugins – they bring a whole new dimension to the final product.

These plugins might help you sell products online, integrate with social media, create stunning photo galleries, manage email subscriptions, or even build a community forum for your visitors. The possibilities are endless, and they can really take your website from basic to extraordinary.

Finding the Right Plugins for You

Just like with any recipe, you don't want to throw everything into the mix without a plan. So, before you go plugin crazy, it's important to consider what specific functionalities you need for your website. What are your goals? What do you want to achieve?

For example, if you're running an online store, you'll need plugins for e-commerce, like **WooCommerce**, **Easy Digital Downloads**, or **Shopify**. These plugins will allow you to create a virtual storefront, manage inventory, process payments, and handle shipping.

If you're a writer or blogger, you might want to consider plugins that help with writing, editing, and scheduling your content, like **Yoast SEO**, **Grammarly**, or **CoSchedule**. These tools can make your content better organized and more visible to your audience.

Popular Plugin Categories

There's a whole universe of plugins out there, categorized by their features and functions. Here are a few popular categories to explore:

E-commerce: These plugins turn your website into a fully functional online store, allowing you to sell physical or digital products.
Security: Security plugins like **Wordfence** and **iThemes Security** help protect your website from hackers and malware. They're crucial for safeguarding your data and keeping your website running smoothly.

Performance Optimization: Plugins like **WP Super Cache** or **W3 Total Cache** can speed up your website's loading time, making it more user-friendly and improving your search engine rankings.
Social Media Integration: Plugins like **Jetpack** , **NextGEN Gallery** , and **Social Media Feather** allow you to connect your website with popular social media platforms like Facebook, Twitter, Instagram, and Pinterest.
Contact Forms: These plugins, like **Contact Form 7** and **WPForms** , make it easy to create custom contact forms for your visitors to get in touch with you.
Content Management: Plugins like **Advanced Custom Fields** , **Gravity Forms** , and **Yoast SEO** help you manage your content in a more organized and efficient way.
Analytics: Plugins like **Google Analytics for WordPress** and **MonsterInsights** let you track your website's performance, providing valuable insights into your audience and how they interact with your site.

Navigating the Plugin Marketplace

Now, how do you find the right plugins? The WordPress plugin directory is a great starting point. It's like a giant online marketplace where you can browse through thousands of free and premium plugins. You can filter by popularity, rating, and features to find the ones that match your needs.

Remember, when choosing a plugin, it's important to consider:

Reputation: Look for plugins with good reviews and high ratings.

Compatibility: Ensure the plugin is compatible with your current WordPress version and theme.
Functionality: Make sure the plugin offers the specific features you need.
Ease of Use: Choose plugins with intuitive interfaces and clear instructions.

Going Beyond the Basics

Once you've got a good foundation with some essential plugins, you can start exploring more advanced options. These plugins can really take your website to the next level and unlock new possibilities.

For example, if you're a photographer, you might want to use a plugin like **NextGEN Gallery** to showcase your work in a stunning and professional way. If you're running a membership site, you might use **MemberPress** to manage subscriptions and restrict access to certain content.

Exploring the Power of Advanced Plugins

Here are some more examples of advanced plugins that can boost your website's functionality and impact:

Membership Sites: Plugins like **MemberPress** and **LearnDash** allow you to create membership sites, offering exclusive content and access to your members. This is perfect for online courses, community forums, or subscription-based content.

E-commerce Powerhouse: WooCommerce is a popular e-commerce plugin that turns your WordPress website into a full-fledged online store. You can add product listings, manage inventory, process payments, and even integrate with shipping providers.

Live Chat Support: Plugins like **WP Live Chat Support** and **Tawk.to** add a live chat feature to your website, allowing you to engage with visitors in real-time and provide instant support.

Advanced SEO: Yoast SEO is a comprehensive SEO plugin that helps you optimize your website for search engines. It analyzes your content, suggests improvements, and provides valuable insights to boost your website's visibility.

Form Builders: Plugins like **Gravity Forms** and **WPForms** are more than just simple contact forms. They allow you to create advanced forms for surveys, donations, registration, and even quizzes.

Calendar Management: Plugins like **The Events Calendar** and **Event Organiser** let you create and manage events, adding a dynamic calendar to your website. This is perfect for businesses, organizations, or individuals who host regular events or workshops.

Booking and Appointment Systems: Plugins like **Bookly** and **Appointment Booking** let you integrate a booking system into your website, allowing users to schedule appointments, book services, or reserve resources.

Image Optimization: Plugins like **Imagify** and **ShortPixel** automatically optimize your images, reducing their file size and improving your website's speed.

Remember, Less Is More

While there are tons of amazing plugins out there, don't feel the need to install every single one. Remember, less is more. Focus on the plugins that directly align with your website's goals and add the most value to your audience.

Just like a good chef knows when to use the right spices in a dish, a savvy website builder understands how to strategically incorporate plugins to enhance the overall user experience.

Unlocking the Full Potential of Your Website

Advanced plugins are the secret weapons in your website toolkit, helping you unlock its full potential and create a truly engaging and impactful online presence. They can help you achieve your goals, connect with your audience, and even generate revenue from your site.

So, don't be afraid to explore the world of advanced plugins and discover what they can do for your website. You might be surprised at the amazing possibilities that are just waiting to be unleashed!

Setting Up Ecommerce Functionality

Now, let's talk about setting up an online store. This is where things get really exciting! Imagine having your own little shop right on your website, selling your amazing crafts, homemade goodies, or anything else you've got a passion for. With WordPress, you can do just that.

First things first, you'll need an e-commerce plugin. Think of it like a magic tool that gives your website the ability to handle online sales. One of the most popular and user-friendly options is WooCommerce. It's like a mini-shopping cart that lets you add products, set prices, manage inventory, and even process payments.

Setting up WooCommerce is a bit like setting up a real-life shop. You'll need to decide on the layout of your store, what products you'll offer, and how you'll showcase them. It's all about creating a visually appealing and easy-to-navigate space where customers can browse and buy.

Here's a step-by-step guide to getting your WooCommerce store up and running:

1. **Installation:** The first step is to install and activate the WooCommerce plugin. Just go to your WordPress dashboard, click on "Plugins," and then "Add New." Search for "WooCommerce," and click "Install Now." Once it's installed, click "Activate." Easy peasy!

2. **Setup Wizard:** WooCommerce will guide you through a setup wizard to configure your store. You'll need to enter some basic information, like your store's name, address, and currency. It's like filling out a form for your new online shop.

3. **Product Creation:** Now it's time to add your products! Click on "Products" in your WordPress dashboard, and then "Add New." Fill out all the details, including product name, description, price, images, and any variations (like different sizes or colors). It's like organizing your shelves in your shop!

4. **Payment Gateway:** You'll need a way to process payments. WooCommerce integrates with popular payment gateways like PayPal, Stripe, and Square. Just go to "WooCommerce" -> "Settings" -> "Payments" and choose the gateway you want to use. It's like getting your cash register ready!

5. **Shipping Settings:** You'll also need to set up your shipping rates. Go to "WooCommerce" -> "Settings" -> "Shipping." You can choose flat rates, based on weight, destination, or even create custom shipping zones. This is like deciding how much it costs to send your packages!

6. **Tax Settings:** You'll also need to configure your tax settings. Go to "WooCommerce" -> "Settings" -> "Tax." You can set up different tax rates for your products based on your location and any applicable sales tax. Just like in the real world, taxes are important!

7. **Store Design:** You can customize the look and feel of your store using themes and plugins. There are tons of beautiful WooCommerce-compatible themes that will make your store look professional and eye-catching. It's like decorating your shop to make it inviting!

8. **Marketing Your Store:** Once your store is set up, it's time to get the word out! Use social media, email marketing, and other marketing strategies to promote your products and

drive traffic to your store. It's like putting up a sign outside your shop to attract customers!

Now, you might be thinking, "WooCommerce sounds a bit complicated, Granny." But trust me, it's really not. With a little patience and guidance, you can easily set up your online store. Think of it like baking a cake. You need the right ingredients (plugins), you need to follow the recipe (setup guide), and then you're good to go. And just like baking, it's rewarding to see your creation come to life.

Here are some additional tips for setting up a successful WooCommerce store:

Clear and concise product descriptions: Tell your customers exactly what they're getting. Use high-quality images and videos to show off your products. Make sure your descriptions are easy to read and understand.
Excellent customer service: Be responsive to customer inquiries and offer helpful support. A happy customer is a returning customer.
Secure payment processing: Use reputable payment gateways to ensure customer trust and security.
Mobile optimization: More and more people shop on their mobile devices. Make sure your store looks great and works flawlessly on all devices.
Promote your store: Don't be shy! Share your store's link on social media, in your email signature, and on any relevant websites.

Remember, building an e-commerce store takes time and effort, but it's a great way to sell your products and grow your business. And who knows, maybe you'll become the next online sensation! So go ahead, Granny, embrace your inner entrepreneur and start selling your amazing creations!

Integrating Social Media

Imagine your website as a bustling town square, filled with interesting people, shops, and events. But how do you get those people to visit and explore? That's where social media comes in! Think of social media as a network of interconnected pathways leading directly to your town square, connecting you with a vast audience eager to discover what you have to offer.

By integrating social media into your website, you're essentially creating a bridge between your online presence and the vibrant world of social media. This bridge allows you to share your website's content with a broader audience, attract new visitors, and foster engagement.

Here's how to build that bridge and leverage the power of social media for your website:

1. Choose Your Social Media Platforms:

The first step is to identify the social media platforms where your target audience hangs out. Just like you wouldn't promote a children's book in a retirement community, it's crucial to choose platforms where your ideal visitors are actively present.

For instance, if you're running a cooking blog aimed at young adults, platforms like Instagram and TikTok might be a better fit than LinkedIn. On the other hand, if you're a business professional sharing industry insights, LinkedIn could be your primary platform.

Don't feel pressured to be everywhere. Start with one or two platforms you feel comfortable using, and gradually expand your presence as you gain confidence.

2. Setting Up Social Media Integration:

Now that you've selected your social media platforms, it's time to connect your website with them. Many website platforms, including WordPress, offer built-in social media integration features, making the process a breeze.

Social Media Buttons: These are small buttons displayed on your website, typically in your header or footer, that allow visitors to quickly share your content on their favorite social media platforms. Think of them as handy "share" buttons for your website's content.
Social Media Feed: This feature allows you to showcase your latest posts from your chosen social media platforms directly on your website, keeping your visitors updated with your most recent content. This creates a dynamic feel and encourages further engagement.
Social Media Login: If you're using a platform like WordPress, you can enable social media login options, allowing visitors to sign up for your website or comment on your posts using their existing social media accounts. This streamlines the process and encourages participation.

3. Creating Engaging Social Media Content:

Once you've integrated your website with social media, it's time to create content that will captivate your audience and entice them to visit your site. Remember, the key is to offer value, build relationships, and spark conversations.

Promote Your Website's Content: Share snippets of your blog posts, highlight your products or services, and tease exciting new features. Include compelling visuals and catchy descriptions to encourage clicks.

Share Behind-the-Scenes Content: Give your audience a glimpse into your process, your team, or your personal journey. This fosters a sense of connection and authenticity, making your brand more relatable.

Engage with Your Followers: Respond to comments, answer questions, and participate in conversations. Think of your social media channels as a virtual town hall where you can interact with your community and build relationships.

4. Cross-Promoting Your Website and Social Media:

Think of your website and social media channels as partners working together to achieve a common goal. Promote your social media profiles on your website, and vice versa. Encourage your followers to visit your site for exclusive content or offers, and link your social media posts back to relevant pages on your website.

5. Track Your Performance and Adapt:

Just like a town square that adapts to the changing needs of its citizens, your social media strategy should be dynamic and responsive to feedback. Use analytics tools to monitor the performance of your social media posts, identify what resonates with your audience, and adapt your strategy accordingly.

Social Media Integration: A Symphony of Connections

Imagine a beautifully orchestrated symphony where each instrument plays a vital role, creating a harmonious whole. Your website is like the conductor, leading the orchestra, while your social media channels are the individual instruments. By integrating your website with social media, you're allowing each element to play its part, creating a vibrant and engaging online experience for your audience.

Think of each social media platform as a different type of music:

Instagram: Visual storytelling, captivating images, and short videos.
Facebook: Sharing news, announcements, and connecting with friends and family.
Twitter: Real-time conversations, breaking news, and sharing opinions.
LinkedIn: Professional networking, industry insights, and career development.

By strategically using these platforms, you can create a symphony of connections, drawing a diverse audience to your website and building a loyal following.

Here are some additional tips for maximizing your social media integration:

Use relevant hashtags: Hashtags are like keywords that help people discover your content. Use them wisely to reach a wider audience.
Run social media contests and giveaways: Encourage participation and generate excitement.
Partner with other brands or influencers: Expand your reach and tap into new audiences.
Don't be afraid to experiment: Try different strategies and see what works best for you.
Be patient and consistent: Building a loyal following takes time and effort.

By integrating social media into your website, you're creating a powerful online ecosystem that attracts visitors, fosters engagement, and ultimately helps you achieve your website goals. Think of it as a vibrant town square, welcoming everyone in with open arms.

Real-Life Examples:

A travel blogger: Uses Instagram to showcase stunning travel photography and links their website for detailed travel guides and itineraries.
A recipe website: Shares delicious-looking food photos on Pinterest and links back to their site for full recipes and cooking instructions.
An online retailer: Uses Facebook to run promotions and customer service inquiries, while their website serves as the online store.

These examples highlight how different businesses and individuals are leveraging social media to enhance their websites and reach a wider audience. By implementing the strategies outlined above, you can unlock the power of social media and make your website a true hub of online activity.

Remember: Don't be afraid to experiment and find what works best for your unique website and target audience. With the right strategies and a bit of creative thinking, you can harness the power of social media to build a thriving online community around your website.

Implementing Contact Forms

Ah, contact forms! They're like the little welcome mats of the digital world, inviting visitors to reach out and connect. You see, contact forms are like digital "get-in-touch" cards. They let folks send you a message without having to reveal their email address right away. It's like sending a postcard, but with more potential for conversation.

Now, imagine this: you've got a beautiful website, all spiffy and organized. But what happens when someone wants to ask a question, share a thought, or maybe even order a dozen of your famous cookies? That's where contact forms come in. They're like friendly little messengers, ready to whisk those messages right into your inbox.

You can create contact forms that look as sleek as your website, with all the right fields for your visitors to fill in. Need a name, email, and message? No problem. Want to know their zip code or favorite color? You can add those fields too!

Here's the fun part: there are a few ways to build your contact form. If you're using a fancy website builder, they often come with a built-in contact form tool. It's like having a pre-made recipe, simple and straightforward. Just click, drag, and drop!

If you're a WordPress whiz, then you've got access to a whole world of plugins. These handy little tools can whip up a contact form in no time. Think of plugins as extra ingredients for your website, adding a little something special.

Let's talk about how to use those contact forms. First, make sure you're using a contact form plugin or your website builder's built-in tool. It's like having a trusty recipe book for all things contact form. Once you've got that set up, you'll find a handy "shortcode" or a bit of code you can copy and paste into your website.

Think of shortcodes as magic words that tell your website to display the contact form right where you want it. You can even add your contact form to a page dedicated to customer service or tuck it away in your "About Us" section.

Now, how about making your contact form look as good as your website? That's where customization comes in. Imagine you're decorating a cake. You can pick out a base flavor, like a vanilla contact form. Then you can add frosting and sprinkles, like changing the colors, adding fields, or arranging the layout.

Most contact form tools let you change things like colors, fonts, and the order of those fields. You can even add a little personality with custom messages, like a friendly "Welcome!" or a fun "Thank you for reaching out!"

Don't forget about those important things: your name, email address, and maybe even a phone number or social media links. They're like the frosting on top, making it easy for people to get in touch with you.

Now, let's talk about the nitty-gritty of making your contact form work like a charm. You'll need to connect your contact form to your email address. It's like sending a letter, but instead of a physical mailbox, you're using your email inbox.

Most contact form plugins and website builders have a way to link your form to your email. Think of it like adding a return address to your letter, ensuring those messages make it to you.

Here's a little trick: If you want to keep things extra organized, you can set up a separate email address just for your contact form. Imagine it like a special inbox just for those messages. This can help you sort through all the emails and keep things tidy.

Remember, your contact form is like a little door that lets people peek inside your website and connect with you. By making it easy to use and visually appealing, you're inviting them to say hello and start a conversation.

Now, go forth and build contact forms that are as delightful as your website!

Now, let's delve into some more specific examples.

A Contact Form for a Bakery

Let's say you're running a delightful bakery. You've got a website showcasing your delicious pastries, but you want people to place orders. Here's how a contact form could help:

Fields:

- **Name:** So you know who's sending the sweet messages!
- **Email:** To reply to the order or send updates.
- **Phone Number:** Just in case there's a quick question or a need to chat about a special order.
- **Order Details:** A space for them to list the goodies they want, maybe with the quantity.

- **Special Instructions:** Maybe they have a preference for gluten-free options or a special delivery request.

Customization:

- **Theme:** Choose a warm, inviting color palette that reflects your bakery's charm.
- **Font:** Pick a font that's easy to read and has a touch of elegance.
- **Message:** A welcoming "Welcome to [Bakery Name]!" with a sweet note about how you love custom orders.

Example:

Imagine your website visitor, Alice, wants to order a dozen of your famous chocolate chip cookies. She fills out the contact form with her name, email, phone number, and details like "1 dozen chocolate chip cookies" in the "Order Details" field. With a click, her request is sent to your inbox, ready for you to whip up those cookies.

A Contact Form for a Blog

Now, let's say you're running a travel blog with lots of amazing stories and helpful tips for adventure seekers. You want to hear from your readers.

Fields:

- **Name:** So you know who's sending the love!
- **Email:** For a personal touch, especially when replying to comments.

- **Subject:** Helps you categorize and quickly understand the message.
- **Message:** A space for your readers to share their travel experiences, ask questions, or offer feedback.

Customization:

- **Theme:** Use a color palette that reflects the adventurous spirit of your blog.
- **Font:** Choose a font that's easy to read and a bit bold, like an adventurer's journal.
- **Message:** Start with a friendly "Hey traveler!" or "We love hearing from you!"

Example:

John, a fellow adventurer, wants to know if you have any tips for hiking the Appalachian Trail. He fills out the contact form with his name, email, and in the "Subject" field, types "Hiking Tips for Appalachian Trail." In the "Message" field, he writes his question about trail supplies or recommended routes. His message lands in your inbox, ready for you to share your expert advice.

A Contact Form for a Local Business

You're running a cozy bookstore with a website that showcases your unique collection. You want to provide a convenient way for customers to ask questions about your inventory, hours, or even request a special book order.

Fields:

- **Name:** To make it personal.
- **Email:** For quick replies.
- **Subject:** Helps you sort and understand the messages quickly.
- **Message:** For inquiries about specific books, store hours, or any other questions they may have.

Customization:

- **Theme:** Use warm, inviting colors that reflect the comforting ambiance of your bookstore.
- **Font:** Pick a font that's easy to read and has a touch of charm.
- **Message:** Start with a welcoming "Welcome to [Bookstore Name]!" and a friendly note about how they can find the books they're looking for.

Example:

Sarah is looking for a specific book that isn't listed on your website. She fills out the form with her name, email, and in the "Subject" field, types "Book Inquiry." In the "Message" field, she writes the title and author of the book she's seeking. Your message lands in your inbox, ready for you to see if you have it in stock or even order it for her.

Remember, your contact form is a bridge between your website and your visitors. By taking the time to create one that's easy to use, visually appealing, and relevant to your website's purpose, you're opening the door to deeper connections and valuable interactions. So, get creative, personalize it, and watch your contact form work its magic!

Using Analytics to Track Performance

You know how you go to the store and you can see how many people have bought a particular item? Well, imagine that for your website! That's what website analytics are all about. It's like a window into how people are interacting with your site, and it can be really useful for making your website better.

Imagine you've just opened up your website, like a brand-new bakery. You're excited to welcome customers, but you want to know what they're buying and how they're finding you. Analytics helps you understand that.

There are lots of different tools you can use to track your website's performance. One of the most popular ones is Google Analytics. It's free and easy to use, and it gives you a lot of great information about your visitors.

With Google Analytics, you can see things like:

Who's visiting your website: You can get an idea of their age, gender, location, and even what kind of devices they're using.
How they found your website: Did they find it through a search engine, a social media post, or a link on another website? This helps you understand what's bringing people to your site.
What pages they're visiting: You can see which pages on your website are getting the most attention and which ones might need some improvements.
How long they're staying: You can see how much time visitors are spending on each page. This can tell you if

they're finding the content engaging or if they're leaving quickly.

What they're clicking on: You can see which links and buttons visitors are clicking. This helps you understand what they're interested in and what might be confusing them.

Think of it like this: You're baking a delicious chocolate cake, and analytics is like those little sprinkles you add on top to make it extra special. It gives you insights that can help you make your website even better.

Here are some real-life examples of how you can use analytics to improve your website:

A grandma who started a recipe blog: Let's say she noticed through analytics that most of her visitors were coming from Pinterest and were interested in vegan recipes. Now she knows to focus on creating more vegan recipes and sharing them on Pinterest to reach a wider audience.

A small business owner who runs an online shop: The owner sees that people are abandoning their shopping carts before checking out. He digs into the data and finds that the checkout process is confusing. He simplifies it, making it easier for customers to complete their purchases.

A hobbyist sharing their travel stories online: Analytics tells him that people are mostly interested in his photos. He starts adding more beautiful pictures to his blog posts and sees a boost in engagement.

But wait, there's more! Analytics isn't just about gathering data; it's also about understanding the data and taking action.

Here are some tips for using analytics effectively:

1. **Set your goals:** Before you even start diving into the data, think about what you want to achieve with your website. Do you want to increase traffic, generate leads, or sell more products? This will help you focus on the metrics that matter most.
2. **Don't get overwhelmed:** Analytics can be a lot of information, so don't get bogged down in the details. Focus on the key metrics that tell you the most about your website's performance.
3. **Look for patterns:** Are there any trends you can identify? For example, you might notice that traffic spikes on weekends or that certain pages are consistently getting more traffic than others. This can help you understand what's working well and what needs improvement.
4. **Don't be afraid to experiment:** Once you've identified some areas that need improvement, try making some changes and then see how it affects your analytics. This is a great way to find what works best for your website.
5. **Be patient:** It takes time to build a successful website. Don't expect to see results overnight. Just keep learning and refining your website based on what you learn from your analytics.

Using analytics is like having a personal coach for your website. It gives you the information you need to make smart decisions and ensure your website is successful.

Now that you understand the power of analytics, you're ready to take your website to the next level. It's like unlocking a secret treasure chest full of knowledge that can help you make your website stand out from the crowd. So, let's dive in and explore the world of analytics together!

Regular Updates and Backups

Okay, Granny's here to talk about keeping your WordPress site in tip-top shape. You've built your website, you've got content flowing, now let's make sure it stays healthy and happy. Imagine your website as a beautiful garden. It needs regular watering, weeding, and a little TLC to flourish.

Think of updates like watering. Just like you wouldn't let your garden go thirsty, your website needs regular updates. WordPress, the software that powers your site, is constantly being improved and updated. These updates fix security holes, improve performance, and add new features. Think of it as giving your website a little boost! Now, imagine those nasty weeds as security threats. They can pop up anytime, and you need to be ready to yank them out. Security updates are like those weed-pulling sessions. They keep your site safe from hackers and nasty bugs.

So, how do you stay on top of these updates? Well, WordPress makes it pretty easy! You'll get notifications in your WordPress dashboard whenever an update is available. Now, I know the sight of "update available" can be a bit daunting, but don't be afraid! Think of it as a little reminder to give your garden a little extra care.

Here's what you need to do:

Back up, back up, back up! Before you update anything, make a backup. It's like taking a picture of your garden before you start digging in. That way, if something goes wrong, you can always restore it to its original state. There are a ton of great backup plugins out there, and many hosting providers offer automatic backups too.

Take it slow and steady. Don't try to update everything at once. Start with the small updates first. If you have a lot of plugins, update them one at a time. This way, if something goes wrong, you'll know exactly which plugin caused the problem.

Don't be afraid to ask for help. If you're feeling overwhelmed, don't hesitate to ask your web developer or a trusted friend for help. They can guide you through the update process and offer troubleshooting tips.

Now, let's talk about those backups. Imagine a power outage in your garden. All your hard work, all those beautiful flowers and vegetables, could be lost. That's why backups are so important. They're like your website's insurance policy. If something goes wrong, like a software glitch or a server problem, you can restore your site to a previous state.

Here are some tips for creating backups:

Frequency is key. How often you back up your site depends on how much content you add and how important your site is. For a busy e-commerce site, daily backups are a good idea. For a personal blog, you might get away with weekly backups.

Multiple locations are better. Never rely on just one backup. Store your backups in multiple locations, such as your computer, a cloud storage service, and even a physical hard drive. That way, even if something happens to one of your backups, you'll have others to fall back on.

Automate where you can. Many plugins and hosting providers offer automated backups. This takes the stress out of backing up, ensuring that your site is always backed up, whether you remember to do it or not.

Don't just back up the files. Back up your entire database as well. This contains all of your website's content, including your posts, pages, comments, and settings. Without a database backup, you'll lose everything.

Test your backups. It's a good idea to test your backups every now and then. Try restoring your site from a backup to make sure it works properly. That way, you'll be confident that your backups are working and that you can recover your website if something goes wrong.

Remember, your website is a valuable investment. It's your online home, your business, your creative outlet. Treat it with the care and attention it deserves. Regular updates and backups are like giving your website a little extra TLC, ensuring that it's healthy and ready to thrive.

Ensuring Website Security

In the digital age, where information travels faster than ever, it's more important than ever to ensure your website is secure. A secure website protects not only your data but also the trust of your visitors. It's like locking your front door; you wouldn't leave it unlocked, would you? The same goes for your website. You don't want hackers sneaking in and stealing your hard work, or worse, causing harm to your visitors.

Think of your website as a cozy cottage in the digital world. It's your space, a place where you share your ideas, stories, or products. But just like a real cottage, it needs protection. Imagine a friendly neighborhood watch keeping an eye out for any suspicious activity. That's what website security is all about – keeping your website safe from unwanted intruders.

Now, you might think, "I'm just a beginner, I don't have anything valuable on my website," but trust me, even a simple blog can be a target for hackers. They're always looking for vulnerable websites to exploit. Think of them as mischievous squirrels trying to find an easy way into your cottage.

So, how do you keep those digital squirrels out? It all comes down to practicing good security habits. It's like building a sturdy fence around your cottage. These habits are like the strong, impenetrable parts of your fence:

1. Keeping Your WordPress Up-to-Date:

Imagine your website's software as the foundation of your cottage. Just like a well-maintained foundation keeps your house safe and sound, keeping your software updated is vital for your website's security.

WordPress, being a popular platform, constantly releases updates to fix any security vulnerabilities that might have been discovered. Think of these updates as security patches that strengthen your website's walls. By keeping WordPress updated, you're essentially patching up any holes in your digital fence, making it harder for hackers to gain access.

It's like getting a fresh coat of paint for your cottage – it not only makes it look better, but it also protects it from the elements. Regularly updating your software is like applying that protective layer, keeping your website strong and secure.

2. Using Strong Passwords:

A strong password is your key to your digital cottage. It's what keeps those mischievous squirrels from unlocking the front door. Just like you wouldn't use a simple "1234" as your door key, a weak password can easily be cracked.

A strong password is like a complex combination lock, difficult to figure out without the right key. Aim for a password that's at least 12 characters long, combining upper and lowercase letters, numbers, and symbols.

Here's a fun way to remember this: think of your password as a secret recipe for your favorite cookies. It should have a combination of ingredients – letters (like flour and sugar), numbers (like the oven temperature), and symbols (like a pinch of salt). Keep it secret, and you'll keep those digital squirrels away.

3. Regularly Changing Your Passwords:

Changing your passwords every few months is like replacing your cottage's locks. It helps prevent anyone who might have gained access to your old password from entering your website.

You might think, "I can remember my password perfectly," but remember, passwords can be leaked, and it's better to be safe than sorry. Just like you change your locks if you suspect someone might have a copy of your key, changing your passwords regularly adds an extra layer of protection.

4. Choosing Strong and Secure Plugins:

Plugins are like the extra features in your cottage, like a fireplace or a cozy reading nook. They enhance your website's functionality. However, some plugins may have security loopholes, just like a poorly built fireplace could pose a fire hazard.

Always choose plugins from reputable developers and make sure they have good reviews. Think of it like checking the manufacturer's warranty on your new furniture – you want to make sure it's reliable and safe. Look for plugins that have frequent updates and security checks.

Just like you wouldn't install a poorly-made fireplace, be cautious about the plugins you add to your website. Choose wisely and always be aware of any potential risks.

5. Backing Up Your Website:

Backing up your website is like creating a blueprint of your cottage. It's a copy of all your data and files, stored safely in case anything happens to your website. Think of it as a digital insurance policy – if something goes wrong, you have a copy to restore your website from.

Imagine a fire breaking out in your cottage. You'd want to have a blueprint so you could rebuild it exactly the same. Website backups work the same way – they give you peace of mind knowing that you can restore your website if it gets compromised.

6. Using Secure Web Hosting:

Choosing a reliable and secure web hosting service is like choosing a solid foundation for your cottage. A secure web hosting provider takes care of the security measures that keep your website safe from external threats. Think of them as the neighborhood security system that keeps your cottage safe.

Always research your web hosting options and choose a provider with a good reputation and a strong security track record. Think of it like asking your neighbors about their recommendations for a security system – you want to make sure you're choosing a trusted and reliable one.

7. Monitoring Website Traffic:

Keeping an eye on your website traffic is like having a watchful neighbor who notices anything unusual going on around your cottage. By monitoring your website's activity, you can identify any suspicious patterns or unusual spikes in traffic.

Think of it like noticing a stranger lurking around your cottage – you'd want to investigate, right? Monitoring your website traffic can help you detect and prevent potential security threats.

8. Enabling Two-Factor Authentication:

Two-factor authentication adds an extra layer of security to your website, like adding a security camera to your cottage. It requires an additional code, usually sent to your phone, whenever you try to log in to your website.

Think of it like having a second lock on your front door – it makes it much harder for anyone to get in without your permission. Enabling two-factor authentication significantly reduces the risk of unauthorized access.

9. Using a Web Application Firewall (WAF):

A WAF is like a security guard stationed at the entrance of your cottage. It acts as a barrier between your website and malicious traffic, preventing harmful attacks.

Think of it as a smart doorman who checks visitors' credentials before letting them into your cottage. A WAF is a proactive defense mechanism that can help protect your website from various threats.

10. Staying Informed About Security Trends:

The digital landscape is constantly evolving, and so are the security threats. It's important to stay updated on the latest security trends and best practices. Just like you would stay informed about neighborhood crime trends, staying updated on website security helps you take preventative measures.

There are numerous resources available, such as online forums, security blogs, and even free online courses, that can help you stay informed about the latest security threats and how to mitigate them. Think of it as attending a community meeting about safety – it keeps you informed and prepared.

By taking these simple steps, you can keep your website secure and safe from hackers. Remember, a secure website is a happy website. It allows you to focus on building great content and interacting with your visitors without worrying about those pesky digital squirrels. So, go ahead and build that sturdy fence around your digital cottage – you'll be glad you did!

Optimizing Site Performance

Now that you have your website up and running, it's essential to keep it in tip-top shape. Just like a well-maintained car runs smoothly and lasts longer, a well-maintained website delivers a great user experience and stays healthy. This involves regular updates, security checks, and a little bit of optimization. Let's dive into the world of website performance, where speed is king!

Imagine you're browsing a website on your phone, waiting for a page to load. You tap impatiently, the seconds tick by, and finally, a blurry image appears. Frustration sets in, and you might just click away to another website. That's the harsh reality of a slow website. It's like a grumpy old car sputtering along, while a fast website is like a sleek sports car, zipping you to your destination quickly and efficiently.

A website's performance is measured by how quickly it loads and responds to user interactions. A slow website can hurt your business, drive away potential customers, and even impact your search engine ranking. Google, the search engine giant, favors websites that load quickly, pushing slower ones further down the search results. This means fewer people will find your website, which translates to fewer visits and, ultimately, fewer leads and sales.

Optimizing for Speed:

So, how do you make your website a speed demon? It's all about optimizing it for performance. Think of it as giving your website a tune-up, making sure every part is working efficiently. There are several key areas to focus on:

1. **Choosing the Right Hosting Provider:**

Just like your website needs a home, it needs a good hosting provider. A reliable and fast hosting provider is like a spacious, well-maintained garage for your website, ensuring it has enough room to breathe and run smoothly. If you're using shared hosting, where multiple websites share resources, your website might be affected by the performance of other websites on the same server. Consider upgrading to a faster option like a VPS or dedicated server, especially if you're running a high-traffic website.

2. **Optimizing Images:**

Images are like the decorations in your website's home. They add visual appeal, but they can also weigh down your website's speed if they're too large. Think of it like this: would you try to carry a giant, heavy sculpture through your house? It would be exhausting, and you wouldn't be able to move around easily. The same goes for your website. Large images can slow down page loading times.

The solution? Use smaller, optimized images. You can use online tools to compress images without sacrificing quality. It's like shrinking your sculpture into a miniature version, making it easier to carry and display.

3. **Minimizing Plugins:**

Plugins are like the tools in your website's toolbox. They add extra features and functionality, but too many plugins can make your website sluggish. Each plugin adds more code and processes, which can slow down your website's loading time. It's like having a toolbox overflowing with tools; it's difficult to find what you need, and the whole thing becomes cumbersome.

Keep your plugin collection lean and mean. Only install plugins that are absolutely necessary for your website's functionality. If you have plugins that you rarely use, consider disabling or removing them.

4. **Caching Your Website:**

Caching is like having a pre-prepared meal in your refrigerator. It saves you time when you're in a hurry. When a visitor comes to your website, the browser downloads all the files needed to display the page. The next time they visit, the browser can access a cached version of the page from their local storage, speeding up the loading time. It's like having a quick and easy meal ready to go, rather than having to cook everything from scratch every time.

Most hosting providers offer caching options, and there are also plugins available for WordPress that can help you optimize caching.

5. **Using a Content Delivery Network (CDN):**

Think of a CDN as a network of servers strategically located around the world. When a visitor accesses your website, the CDN delivers the content from the server closest to them. It's like having multiple copies of your website stored in different locations, making it faster and easier for people to access it, no matter where they are.

A CDN can significantly improve your website's performance, especially if you have a global audience.

6. Choosing a Fast Theme:

Your website's theme is like the overall design and layout of your home. It sets the tone and style for your website. Some themes are more complex and feature-rich than others, which can affect performance. A heavy theme with lots of animations and effects might be beautiful, but it can also slow down your website.

Choose a theme that is lightweight and optimized for speed. There are many beautiful and responsive themes available that are also efficient.

7. Minimizing Code:

Every website is built using code. Just like a well-written book is concise and to the point, a well-written codebase is efficient and streamlined. Too much code can lead to a bloated and slow website.

You can minimize your code by removing unnecessary comments, combining CSS and JavaScript files, and using a minifier tool to shrink the file size.

8. Optimizing Database Queries:

Your website's database is like a library that stores all the information about your content. When you request a page, your database needs to fetch the information from the library. Too many database queries can slow down your website, as it has to search through the library too many times.

You can optimize your database queries by using indexes to speed up searches, reducing the number of unnecessary queries, and using a database caching plugin.

Monitoring Your Website's Performance:

You can use various tools to monitor your website's performance and identify areas for improvement. It's like having a speedometer for your website, letting you know if it's running fast or slow.

Google PageSpeed Insights: This free tool from Google analyzes your website's speed and provides recommendations for improvement.

GTmetrix: This tool offers a detailed analysis of your website's performance, including suggestions for optimization.

Pingdom: This tool provides insights into your website's speed and performance, including a breakdown of individual page load times.

Website Speed Test: This tool provides a simple and quick way to test your website's loading speed.

Google Analytics: This tool can help you track how quickly your website loads for different visitors, allowing you to identify potential performance issues.

By optimizing your website for speed, you can improve the user experience, attract more visitors, and boost your search engine ranking. It's like giving your website a boost of energy, allowing it to run smoothly and efficiently. So, take the time to tune up your website, and watch it soar to new heights!

Managing User Roles and Permissions

Managing user roles and permissions in WordPress might sound like a technical hurdle, but trust me, it's a vital step to keep your website secure and organized. Think of it as adding locks to your online home, allowing only trusted individuals to access specific areas.

You might be wondering, "Why do I even need user roles?" Well, imagine you're creating a blog with your family, where each member contributes articles. You wouldn't want everyone having access to sensitive information like financial details, right?

That's where user roles come in. They're like digital badges that determine who can do what on your website. In WordPress, there are several default roles:

Administrator: This is the ultimate boss with full access to everything – editing, managing users, changing themes, and more. It's typically reserved for the website owner.
Editor: This role can manage all content on the website, including posts, pages, and media. They can also create new users, but can't modify user roles or site settings.
Author: This role is perfect for content creators who can write and publish their own posts, but they can't manage other users or change website settings.
Contributor: This role is for those who can write posts but need an Editor's approval to publish them.
Subscriber: This role is for basic users who can only log in and access certain parts of the website, usually for things like commenting or subscribing to newsletters.

Now, let's say you're creating a website for your local gardening club. You might assign different roles based on member responsibilities:

Administrator: You, the club president, will hold this role to oversee everything.
Editor: The club's newsletter editor will manage all the content for the club's website, ensuring everything is informative and up to date.
Author: Members who write blog posts about their gardening experiences will have this role.
Contributor: New members who want to contribute can write posts, which will be reviewed by the editor before publishing.
Subscriber: Non-member visitors to the website will be automatically assigned this role, allowing them to access general information about the club but not make any changes.

However, the default roles might not always be enough. You might need to adjust them based on your specific website needs. For example, you might want to create a "Gallery Manager" role to allow someone to upload and manage images, or a "Social Media Manager" role to handle the website's social media integration.

Here's how to customize roles and permissions in WordPress:

1. **Log in to your WordPress dashboard:** This is your control center, accessible through your website address followed by "/wp-admin".
2. **Navigate to "Users" > "Roles":** This will open a page with a list of default roles.
3. **Click on "Add New Role":** This allows you to create a completely new role.

4. **Give your role a name:** Be descriptive and clear, such as "Event Coordinator" or "Social Media Manager."
5. **Select permissions:** You'll see a long list of capabilities associated with each role. Select the ones that are relevant for your new role.
6. **Click "Add Role":** Congratulations! You've created a custom role.
7. **Assign the role to users:** Go to "Users" > "All Users," and select the user you want to assign the new role to. Click "Edit" and change their role from the dropdown menu.

A Few Key Tips for Managing User Roles:

Start Simple: Don't overcomplicate things by creating too many custom roles initially. Stick to the default roles unless you have specific reasons to customize them.
Define Clear Responsibilities: Before assigning roles, make sure you clearly understand what each user is responsible for. This helps prevent confusion and overlapping tasks.
Review Regularly: As your website grows, take some time to review the roles and permissions to ensure they still fit your current needs.
Security First: Be cautious about granting access to sensitive areas. Consider using the "Subscriber" role for visitors who don't need to make changes.

Consider this: Imagine you've added a "Volunteer Coordinator" role to your gardening club website. This role would allow the volunteer coordinator to manage a page with volunteer opportunities, add new volunteers to the database, and communicate with volunteers through email. This role specifically focuses on volunteer management, ensuring that the coordinator has the necessary permissions without granting unnecessary access to other parts of the website.

Managing user roles and permissions in WordPress might seem complex at first, but with a bit of understanding and planning, it becomes a powerful tool for maintaining your website's security and organization. Remember, it's about empowering the right people to do the right things, keeping your website running smoothly and efficiently.

Handling Technical Issues

Even with regular updates and backups, technical issues can pop up. It's like having a well-maintained car; you still might encounter a flat tire or a flickering light. No matter how careful you are, unexpected things happen in the world of websites.

Here are some common technical issues you might face and how to troubleshoot them:

Website Down or Loading Slowly:

The Most Basic Check: Your Internet Connection

The first thing to check is whether your internet connection is working properly. Try visiting other websites to rule out an issue on your end.

Website Hosting Issues:

- **Server Downtime:** Your website might be down due to server maintenance or a technical problem at your hosting provider. Check your hosting company's status page or contact their support for updates.
- **Resource Exhaustion:** If your website is using too much server resources (like memory or CPU), it might become slow or unresponsive. Contact your hosting provider to discuss potential solutions, like upgrading your hosting plan.
- **Database Issues:** A malfunctioning database can also lead to website downtime. Check your hosting provider's

documentation or contact their support if you suspect database problems.

Plugin Conflicts:

- Plugins are like add-ons that enhance your website's functionality. Sometimes, they clash with each other or with your theme, causing website errors. If you've recently installed a new plugin, try deactivating it and see if the issue resolves.

Theme Issues:

- Themes control the look and feel of your website. Similar to plugins, themes can sometimes have conflicts that affect website performance. Try switching to a default WordPress theme (like Twenty Twenty-Three) to see if the issue disappears.

DNS Problems:

- Domain Name System (DNS) records link your domain name to your website's server. If there's a DNS error, visitors might not be able to find your site. Contact your domain registrar or hosting provider for assistance with DNS settings.

Broken Links:

Broken Links and User Experience:

- Broken links are like dead ends on your website. They can frustrate visitors and harm your website's credibility.

How to Find Broken Links:

- **Plugins:** There are many plugins available (like Broken Link Checker or Broken Link Status Checker) that automatically scan your website for broken links. These plugins will provide you with a list of broken links and the pages where they occur, making it easy to fix them.
- **Manual Checking:** You can also check for broken links manually by clicking through your site and looking for links that don't work.
- **Website Analytics:** Tools like Google Analytics can also help you identify broken links by tracking user behavior. Look for pages with high bounce rates or low time on page, which could indicate broken links that are causing users to leave quickly.

Fixing Broken Links:

- Once you've identified broken links, you can either update them with the correct URL or remove them completely. If you're removing links, make sure to replace them with relevant content or link them to a similar page on your site.

Error Messages:

Error Messages Can Be Helpful:

- Error messages, while frustrating, often provide valuable clues to help you diagnose and fix website problems.

Common Error Messages and Their Meanings:

- **404 Not Found:** This means the requested page doesn't exist. It could be a typo in the URL, a missing page, or a broken link.
- **500 Internal Server Error:** This error indicates a problem with the server, which could be caused by a variety of issues.
- **403 Forbidden:** You don't have permission to access the requested resource. This could be a security measure, a problem with your website's configuration, or a corrupted file.
- **White Screen of Death:** This dreaded screen means WordPress can't load properly. It can be caused by plugin conflicts, theme issues, corrupted files, or insufficient server resources.

Troubleshooting Error Messages:

- **Check Your Website's Error Log:** Most hosting providers provide access to your website's error log, which can be a valuable resource for understanding why your website is experiencing errors.
- **Deactivate Plugins and Themes:** If you're experiencing an error, try deactivating all your plugins and switching to a default theme. If the error disappears, you know the problem is related to either a plugin or your theme.
- **Contact Your Hosting Provider:** If you're unable to resolve the issue, don't hesitate to reach out to your hosting provider's support team for assistance.

Security Issues:

Staying Vigilant:

- Security is crucial for any website. Hackers are constantly looking for vulnerabilities to exploit, so it's essential to stay vigilant.

Common Security Threats:

- **Malware Infections:** Malware can infect your website and compromise its functionality, steal data, or redirect users to malicious websites.
- **Brute Force Attacks:** Hackers might try to guess your website's login credentials by repeatedly entering different combinations.
- **Cross-Site Scripting (XSS):** This attack allows attackers to inject malicious scripts into your website, which can steal user information or compromise the site's integrity.
- **SQL Injection:** This attack involves manipulating database queries to gain unauthorized access to your website's data.

Protecting Your Website:

- **Install a Security Plugin:** Use a reputable security plugin (like Wordfence, iThemes Security, or Sucuri) to protect your website from common threats. These plugins offer features like malware scanning, firewall protection, and brute force attack prevention.
- **Strong Passwords:** Choose strong, unique passwords for your website's logins and other accounts.
- **Keep Software Updated:** Regularly update your WordPress core, themes, and plugins. These updates often include security patches that fix vulnerabilities.
- **Two-Factor Authentication:** Enable two-factor authentication for your website's login and any other sensitive accounts. This adds an extra layer of security by requiring a code from your phone in addition to your password.

- **Back Up Your Website Regularly:** Regular backups are crucial for recovering your website if it's affected by a security breach or other technical issues.

Image Optimization and Website Performance:

Optimize Images:

- **Compression:** Compress your images to reduce their file size without sacrificing quality. There are online tools and plugins (like ShortPixel Image Optimizer or Smush) that can help you compress images.
- **Format:** Use the most efficient image format for your needs. JPEGs are generally best for photographs, while PNGs are better for images with transparent backgrounds or sharp edges.
- **Image Dimensions:** Resize images to fit the dimensions they'll be displayed at on your website. Large images can slow down your site's loading times.

Caching:

- **Caching Plugins:** Use a caching plugin (like WP Super Cache or W3 Total Cache) to store copies of your website's pages and deliver them to visitors more quickly.
- **Server-Side Caching:** Your hosting provider might offer caching features as well, which can further improve website performance.

Website Performance Tools:

- **Google PageSpeed Insights:** This tool analyzes your website's performance and suggests ways to improve its

speed.
- **Pingdom:** This tool provides detailed insights into your website's loading times and offers suggestions for optimization.

Mobile Responsiveness:

A Mobile-First World:

- Today, more people browse the internet on their mobile devices than on desktops. A website that isn't mobile-friendly can result in a poor user experience, leading to frustrated visitors and potential loss of business.

How to Make Your Website Mobile-Responsive:

- **Mobile-Friendly Themes and Plugins:** Choose a theme or install a plugin that is designed to be mobile-responsive. These themes and plugins automatically adjust your website's layout to fit different screen sizes.
- **Responsive Design:** Make sure your website's content and layout adapt to different screen sizes. Use fluid grids and relative units in your CSS to ensure a consistent experience across devices.
- **Mobile Testing:** Regularly test your website on different mobile devices to ensure it displays correctly and is easy to navigate.

Staying Up to Date with Website Trends:

A Dynamic Landscape:

- The world of websites is constantly evolving. New technologies, design trends, and SEO best practices emerge regularly. It's essential to stay up to date to keep your website relevant and engaging.

How to Keep Up with Trends:

- **Follow Industry Blogs and Websites:** Subscribe to reputable websites and blogs (like Moz, Search Engine Journal, or Smashing Magazine) that cover website design, development, and marketing trends.
- **Attend Webinars and Conferences:** These events offer valuable insights from industry experts and can help you stay on top of the latest technologies and strategies.
- **Join Online Communities:** Connect with other website owners and developers in online forums and groups to exchange ideas, share experiences, and learn from one another.

Seeking Help When You Need It:

Don't Be Afraid to Ask for Assistance:

- Even the most experienced website owners encounter issues they can't solve on their own. It's okay to seek help from a trusted friend, fellow website builder, or a professional web developer.

Finding Reliable Help:

- **Web Development Forums:** These forums are excellent resources for getting help from experienced web developers.
- **WordPress Support:** WordPress offers a comprehensive support system, including official documentation, forums, and a dedicated support team.
- **Freelance Platforms:** Websites like Upwork or Fiverr allow you to connect with freelance web developers who can help you with a wide range of tasks.

Remember, building a website is a journey, and you'll likely encounter a few bumps along the way. But with patience, persistence, and a willingness to learn, you can overcome technical challenges and create a website you're proud of.

Effective Marketing Strategies

Now that you've got your website up and running, it's time to start attracting visitors and building a community around your online space. The most effective way to do this is through marketing! Don't worry, you don't need to be a marketing whiz to get started. We'll cover some basic yet powerful strategies that you can implement right away.

Think of marketing like a giant picnic basket filled with delicious goodies. You've got your website, which is the basket itself. Now, we need to fill it with yummy treats to entice people to come closer and take a bite. These tasty treats are your marketing strategies.

The Power of Email Marketing

Imagine having a direct line to your audience, a way to reach them directly in their inbox. That's the magic of email marketing! It's like sending personalized postcards, but instead of paper, you're using digital mail.

How does it work? You create a list of people interested in your website's content. This list can be built by offering a freebie, like a downloadable guide or a discount code, in exchange for their email address. Once you have their email, you can send them regular updates about your website, new blog posts, special offers, or even just a friendly "hello!"

But remember, just like you wouldn't send a stranger a bunch of unsolicited mail, you need to be mindful of what you're sending to your email subscribers.

Keep it personal: Tailor your emails to your audience's interests. If you're a baking blogger, don't send emails about gardening!

Offer valuable content: Provide useful information, tips, or behind-the-scenes insights that your audience will actually find helpful.

Don't bombard them: Send emails sparingly, perhaps once a week or even less frequently. Too many emails can make people feel overwhelmed and unsubscribe.

Unleashing the SEO Beast

SEO stands for Search Engine Optimization. Think of it as making your website visible to search engines like Google, Bing, and Yahoo. When someone searches for something online, like "best apple pie recipe" or "how to build a website", SEO helps your website show up in the search results.

The key to SEO is understanding what people are searching for and making sure your website provides the information they're looking for. Imagine your website as a cozy bookstore. To attract readers, you need to organize your books in a way that makes it easy for them to find what they want.

Here are some basic SEO tips:

Choose relevant keywords: Research what people are searching for related to your website's content. Use those keywords naturally in your website copy, blog posts, and page titles.

Optimize your website's content: Make sure your website's text is clear, concise, and easy to read. Use short paragraphs, headings, and subheadings to break up the text and make it visually appealing.

Use alt text for images: When you upload images to your website, add descriptive alt text. This helps search engines understand the content of your images.

Building a Thriving Community

Your website isn't just a place to share information; it's an opportunity to connect with people who share your interests. Building a community around your website takes time and effort, but it's incredibly rewarding.

Engage with your readers: Respond to comments on your blog posts and social media updates. Ask questions and encourage discussions.

Host online events: Consider hosting webinars, online workshops, or Q&A sessions related to your website's topics.

Create a sense of belonging: Make your website a welcoming and inclusive space where people feel comfortable sharing their thoughts and experiences.

Think of your website as a warm and inviting living room. You want people to feel comfortable coming in, settling down, and chatting with their friends.

Monetizing Your Website

Once you have a strong audience and a thriving community, you might want to explore ways to monetize your website. This means turning your passion project into a source of income.

Here are some common ways to monetize a website:

Affiliate marketing: Partner with brands or companies that align with your website's content and promote their products or services in your blog posts or website pages. You earn a commission for every sale made through your affiliate links.
Display advertising: Allow companies to place advertisements on your website. You get paid based on the number of impressions (times the ad is shown) or clicks.
Selling products or services: If you have your own products or services to sell, your website is a great platform to showcase them. This could be anything from digital products like ebooks or online courses to physical goods like handmade crafts or merchandise.

It's important to remember that monetizing your website should be done ethically and transparently. Always be upfront with your readers about any affiliate relationships or paid advertising you have. And most importantly, focus on providing value and building a strong community before trying to generate income.

Remember, You're Not Alone

Building a website and growing its audience is a journey, not a destination. There will be ups and downs, moments of frustration, and times when you feel like giving up. But don't be discouraged! Remember, there are countless resources available to support you, from online communities and forums to blogs and tutorials.

And most importantly, remember that you're not alone. Many people have started their own websites with no prior experience, and they've been incredibly successful. So, don't be afraid to experiment, learn from your mistakes, and have fun along the way!

Remember, it's all about sharing your passion and connecting with others. You've got this!

Utilizing Email Marketing

Now, let's talk about **email marketing**, a powerful tool for building relationships with your website visitors and keeping them engaged. Imagine email marketing as a friendly letter you send to your visitors, keeping them updated on your latest blog posts, new products, or exciting announcements. It's a personal touch that helps you nurture a loyal following.

Setting up Your Email Marketing System

First things first, you'll need a way to collect email addresses from your visitors. You can do this by adding a simple signup form on your website. Many website builders and platforms, like WordPress, offer built-in forms or plugins to make it easy.

Consider placing your signup form strategically. It's often effective to place it prominently on your homepage or landing page. You can also offer a special incentive, like a free ebook or discount, to encourage people to sign up.

Once you have your email addresses, you'll need an email marketing platform to manage your list and send emails. There are many options available, both free and paid, with features that cater to different needs. Some popular choices include Mailchimp, Constant Contact, and Campaigner.

When choosing an email marketing platform, consider factors like ease of use, features, pricing, and customer support. Many platforms offer free plans for smaller lists, which can be a great starting point.

Crafting Engaging Email Content

Now, let's talk about the heart of email marketing – creating compelling content that your subscribers will actually want to read. Think of your emails as opportunities to connect with your audience and offer them value.

Here are some email content ideas:

New blog posts: Promote your latest blog posts, providing a snippet of what readers can expect.
Exclusive content: Offer subscribers access to exclusive content, such as behind-the-scenes insights, free downloads, or early access to promotions.
Product updates: If you have an e-commerce store, keep subscribers informed about new products, sales, or special offers.
Newsletters: Create a regular newsletter with curated content, industry news, or updates on your website.
Personal stories: Share personal stories or anecdotes that connect with your audience and build a sense of community.

Here are some tips for writing engaging emails:

Keep it concise and to the point: Your readers are busy, so get to the point quickly and make your emails easy to scan.
Use a friendly and conversational tone: Write like you're talking to a friend, keeping your emails personal and engaging.
Include a clear call to action: Tell your readers what you want them to do, whether it's clicking a link, visiting your website, or making a purchase.
Use visuals to enhance your emails: Images, videos, and GIFs can break up your text and make your emails more visually appealing.
Proofread carefully: Before you hit send, make sure to proofread your emails for typos and grammatical errors.

Segmenting Your Email List

As your email list grows, it's a good idea to segment it into different groups based on your subscribers' interests, demographics, or behavior. This allows you to send more targeted and relevant emails that are more likely to resonate with your audience.

For example, you could create segments for:

Blog readers: Send emails about new blog posts or related content.
Product buyers: Promote new products or discounts to those who have purchased from you before.
Location: If your business has a local focus, send targeted emails to subscribers in your area.
Interests: If your audience has diverse interests, you can create segments based on specific topics.

Tracking and Analyzing Email Performance

Just like with any other marketing effort, it's essential to track and analyze your email marketing results. Most email marketing platforms provide analytics that show you:

Open rates: The percentage of subscribers who opened your email.
Click-through rates: The percentage of subscribers who clicked on a link in your email.
Bounce rates: The percentage of emails that couldn't be delivered.
Unsubscribe rates: The percentage of subscribers who unsubscribed from your list.

By tracking these metrics, you can identify what's working well and what needs improvement. This data can help you refine your email strategy and improve your results over time.

Email Marketing Best Practices

To ensure your email marketing efforts are successful, follow these best practices:

Get permission before sending emails: Always obtain consent from your subscribers before adding them to your email list.
Send emails at the right time: Experiment with different sending times to see when your subscribers are most engaged.
Respect your subscribers' time: Keep your emails concise and avoid sending too many emails.
Make it easy to unsubscribe: Include a clear unsubscribe link in all your emails.
Comply with all laws and regulations: Familiarize yourself with the relevant laws and regulations regarding email marketing in your region.

Building Relationships Through Email Marketing

Email marketing is more than just sending promotional emails. It's about building relationships with your audience, providing valuable content, and nurturing a sense of community. By consistently delivering high-quality content and engaging with your subscribers, you can build trust and loyalty, leading to increased website traffic, sales, and brand awareness.

As you gain more experience with email marketing, you'll discover new strategies and techniques that work best for your website. Keep experimenting, track your results, and adapt your approach based on what you learn. And remember, email marketing is an ongoing process – it takes time and effort to build a successful email list and engage your subscribers effectively.

Email marketing is an essential tool for anyone who wants to grow their website's reach and build a strong online presence. With careful planning, engaging content, and consistent efforts, you can use email marketing to connect with your audience, build relationships, and achieve your website goals.

Leveraging SEO for Growth

Now, let's talk about **SEO**, which stands for **Search Engine Optimization**. Think of SEO as a magic spell that helps your website get noticed by those all-knowing internet giants like Google, Bing, and Yahoo. The more your website shows up in search results, the more people will find it, right? It's like having a billboard on the busiest digital highway in the world!

Here's the thing: those search engines have little robots called **crawlers** that constantly roam the internet, checking out websites and indexing them. These crawlers look at a website's content, structure, and technical aspects to understand what it's about and how relevant it is to search queries.

So, how do we make our website irresistible to these crawlers and, ultimately, to our target audience? That's where SEO comes in. It's all about making your website **search engine-friendly**, so it gets a good ranking in those search results.

Keyword Research: Finding the Right Words

Imagine you're looking for a new recipe online. You might type in "chocolate chip cookies" or "easy lasagna recipe." Those words are **keywords**, the terms people use to find information online. Your website needs to use the right keywords to attract the right audience.

Keyword research is the process of identifying the words and phrases that people are searching for in your niche. It's like eavesdropping on the internet to understand what people are looking for. There are various tools available, both free and paid, to help you with this.

For example, Google Keyword Planner is a great free tool. You can enter your website's topic or a specific keyword and see how often people search for it, the competition for that keyword, and related keywords you might want to consider.

Once you have a list of relevant keywords, it's time to sprinkle them strategically throughout your website.

On-Page SEO: Optimizing Your Website Content

On-page SEO is all about making sure your website content is optimized for search engines. Here are some key things to keep in mind:

Keyword Placement: Use your keywords in your website's title, headings, descriptions, and content. But remember, it's about quality, not just stuffing keywords everywhere. Search engines are smart; they can tell if you're trying to trick them!
Content Quality: Create high-quality, informative, and engaging content that provides value to your audience. Search engines prioritize websites that offer helpful information and a good user experience. Think about it: if you were searching for a recipe, would you trust a website with a poorly written, vague recipe or one with detailed instructions and beautiful photos?
URL Optimization: Make your website's URLs clear and concise, incorporating relevant keywords. Avoid long, confusing URLs with random numbers and letters. For example, "www.yourwebsite.com/delicious-chocolate-chip-cookies" is much better than "www.yourwebsite.com/123456789/recipe.html."
Image Optimization: Optimize your images by using descriptive file names and adding alt tags. Alt tags are short descriptions of the images that help search engines understand what they're about. They're also important for accessibility, as they allow screen readers to describe the images to users with visual impairments.

Off-Page SEO: Building Your Website's Authority

Off-page SEO focuses on building your website's reputation and credibility in the online world. It's about getting other websites to link to yours, which is like getting a vote of confidence from the internet community.

Link Building: Building backlinks is a crucial aspect of off-page SEO. Backlinks are links from other websites pointing to yours. Think of them like recommendations or endorsements. The more backlinks your website has, the more authoritative it appears to search engines.

Guest Blogging: Write guest posts on other relevant websites in your niche. This is a great way to reach a new audience and get backlinks to your website. Just make sure to link back to your website from your guest posts.

Social Media Marketing: Engage on social media and share your website's content. Social media can help you build an online community and get people talking about your website. Use relevant hashtags to reach a wider audience.

Local SEO: If you have a brick-and-mortar business, local SEO is essential to ensure you show up in local search results. This includes listing your business on Google My Business, adding your business address to your website, and getting local citations on online directories.

Technical SEO: Ensuring a Smooth Ride for Crawlers

Technical SEO is about making sure your website is technically sound and easy for search engines to crawl and understand.

Mobile Friendliness: Ensure your website is mobile-friendly. More and more people are browsing the internet on their smartphones, so a responsive website that adapts to different screen sizes is a must. Google even prioritizes mobile-friendly websites in its search results.

Page Speed: Website speed is crucial for user experience and SEO. Slow loading times can lead to frustrated visitors and lower search rankings. Optimize your website images, use a fast hosting provider, and minimize the use of unnecessary scripts and plugins.

Sitemaps: A sitemap is like a map of your website that helps search engines understand its structure. It lists all your website's pages, making it easier for crawlers to index your content.

Structured Data: Structured data is a way to give search engines extra information about your website's content. It's like adding a "this is what it is" label to your pages. You can use structured data to mark up content such as recipes, products, events, and reviews, helping search engines understand and display your content better.

Tracking Your Progress and Making Adjustments

Remember, SEO is an ongoing process, not a one-time fix. You need to track your progress and make adjustments as needed.

Google Analytics: This is a free tool from Google that provides valuable insights into your website's traffic, user behavior, and performance. You can see how people are finding your website, what pages they're visiting, and how long they stay on each page.

Google Search Console: This is another free tool from Google that helps you monitor your website's search performance. You can see which keywords are driving traffic to your website, any errors that search engines are encountering, and how your website appears in search results.

By regularly analyzing these data points, you can identify areas where you can improve your SEO efforts. For example, if you notice a decline in traffic for a specific keyword, you might need to update your website content to include more relevant keywords or address the specific search intent behind that keyword.

The Power of SEO: Building a Sustainable Online Presence

SEO can seem like a lot to take in, but remember, it's a journey, not a sprint. Start by focusing on the basics and gradually add more advanced techniques as you gain experience.

By taking the time to learn about SEO and applying these strategies, you can create a website that attracts the right audience and thrives in the competitive online landscape. It's like building a strong foundation that will support your website's growth and success for years to come.

Think of it like this: **SEO is like a secret sauce that makes your website irresistible to search engines and visitors alike.** It's the key to unlocking your website's full potential and reaching a vast audience online.

Building Community and Engagement

Building a website is like baking a delicious cake – you need the right ingredients, a good recipe, and a touch of love to create something truly special. But just like a cake needs frosting to make it irresistible, your website needs engagement to make it truly successful. You've put in the time and effort to build a beautiful website, filled with content you're proud of, but it's only half the battle. Now, it's time to bring your website to life by cultivating a vibrant community and encouraging visitors to stay engaged.

Imagine your website as a cozy coffee shop. You've got the perfect ambiance, delicious treats, and a welcoming atmosphere, but what truly brings people back is the sense of community – the lively conversations, the shared laughter, and the feeling of belonging.

Building a strong online community is all about fostering connection, creating a space where people feel welcome to share their thoughts, ask questions, and interact with each other. Think of it as a virtual gathering place where your website becomes a hub for like-minded individuals to connect and share their experiences.

Here are a few ways to foster a thriving community on your website:

1. Embrace the Power of Comments:

Comments are the lifeblood of online engagement. Imagine a bustling coffee shop where everyone is engaged in lively conversations. Comments on your website serve the same purpose. They provide a platform for your readers to share their thoughts, ask questions, and connect with each other.

Encourage active participation:
- Make it easy for visitors to leave comments. Keep the comment form simple and user-friendly.
- Respond to comments promptly and personally. Show your visitors that you value their input and are actively listening.
- Ask thought-provoking questions to spark conversations and encourage further discussion.
- Moderate comments to ensure a positive and respectful environment.

2. Harness the Strength of Social Media:

Social media is a powerful tool for building community and expanding your reach. It's like having a billboard in a busy city square, allowing you to connect with a broader audience and engage with potential visitors.

Integrate seamlessly:
- Include social media sharing buttons on your website. Make it easy for visitors to share your content on their favorite platforms.
- Create engaging social media content that aligns with your website's theme and target audience.
- Promote your website on your social media channels and encourage followers to visit.
- Interact with followers on social media, respond to comments, and build relationships.

3. Embrace the Community of Forums:

Forums are like online town squares, buzzing with activity and offering a platform for people to connect and share their expertise. Imagine your website as a forum for your passion, where you can gather a community of like-minded individuals to exchange ideas, seek advice, and support each other.

Cultivate a welcoming space:
- Create a forum on your website dedicated to specific topics related to your content.
- Establish clear guidelines for respectful and constructive discussions.
- Encourage active participation by asking questions and engaging in conversations.
- Moderate the forum to ensure a safe and inclusive environment.

4. Host Online Events and Gatherings:

Online events and gatherings are like virtual coffee mornings, bringing people together for a shared experience. These events can be webinars, online workshops, Q&A sessions, or even virtual book clubs.

Connect and engage:
- Host regular online events that are relevant to your website's theme and audience.
- Promote your events on social media and your website.
- Make it easy for participants to register and attend.
- Engage with participants during and after the event, fostering a sense of connection.

5. Personalize the Experience with Email Marketing:

Email marketing is like sending personalized postcards to your website visitors, keeping them informed about your latest updates and engaging them in meaningful conversations. Think of it as a way to nurture your relationship with your audience and keep them connected to your website.

Build relationships:
- Create a newsletter that delivers valuable content, exclusive updates, and behind-the-scenes insights.
- Personalize your email campaigns by segmenting your audience and tailoring content to their interests.
- Include calls to action to encourage engagement and drive traffic to your website.
- Monitor email engagement and refine your strategies based on feedback.

6. Encourage User-Generated Content:

User-generated content is like inviting your website visitors to contribute their own recipes to your virtual cookbook. It gives them a voice, encourages their participation, and adds a unique flavor to your online community.

Let your visitors share:
- Create a platform for visitors to share their own stories, experiences, and perspectives.
- Host contests and challenges that encourage user-generated content.
- Recognize and celebrate valuable contributions from your community members.

7. Run Contests and Giveaways:

Contests and giveaways are like offering free samples in your coffee shop – a fun way to attract new visitors and reward your loyal community members. They create excitement, generate buzz, and encourage participation.

Reward engagement:

- Host contests and giveaways that are relevant to your website's theme and audience.
- Promote your contests and giveaways on social media and your website.
- Choose winners fairly and recognize their contributions.

Building a thriving online community is an ongoing journey, but the rewards are well worth the effort. It's about fostering a sense of connection, encouraging participation, and creating a space where your visitors feel valued and heard. Remember, your website is more than just a collection of pages; it's a platform to build relationships, share knowledge, and create a lasting impact. So, go forth and cultivate a vibrant community that will make your website truly come alive!

Monetizing Your Website

Now that you have built a fantastic website and are ready to share it with the world, you might be thinking, "How can I make this website work for me?" Well, grandma's got you covered! There are lots of creative ways to monetize your website, turning it into a source of income or a valuable asset for your business.

Advertising

One of the most common ways to make money online is through advertising. Think of those little banners you see on websites, those are ads! These are often paid for by companies who want to reach a wider audience. Now, you don't have to become a billboard for every company out there. You can be selective.

Choose relevant ads: Pick ads that fit your website's content and appeal to your audience. If your website is about gardening, ads for gardening tools would be a perfect fit.
Use a network: Don't try to handle advertising yourself. There are advertising networks that connect websites with advertisers. They handle all the technical stuff, like placing ads and tracking clicks. Popular networks include Google AdSense, Media.net, and PropellerAds.
Don't overdo it: Too many ads will overwhelm visitors and drive them away. Keep ads subtle and balanced so they don't distract from your content.

Affiliate Marketing

Imagine this: You write a blog post about your favorite kitchen gadgets. You include links to where your readers can buy those gadgets. When a reader clicks your link and makes a purchase, you get a commission! This is called affiliate marketing.

Partner with relevant brands: Find brands that align with your website's niche. If you have a travel blog, partner with airlines, hotels, or travel agencies.
Promote products you believe in: Don't just recommend anything for a commission. Share products and services you genuinely love and would recommend to your own family.
Use clear disclosure: Be upfront about affiliate relationships. Let your readers know that you may earn a commission if they click a link.

Selling Products and Services

Your website can be a storefront for your own products and services. It's like having a little shop online!

Create digital products: eBooks, online courses, templates, or even music and art can be sold through your website.
Offer services: If you have skills like writing, editing, graphic design, or web development, you can offer your services on your website.
Set up a shopping cart: You'll need a way for customers to purchase your products or services. Platforms like Etsy, Shopify, or even WordPress plugins can help you set up a shopping cart.

Membership Site

Imagine building a community around your website, a special club where members get exclusive content, discounts, and access to a private forum. This is what a membership site can do!

Offer exclusive content: Provide members with valuable content that isn't available to the public.
Create a community: Build a forum or group where members can connect and interact with each other.
Offer different tiers: Have different membership levels with varying benefits and costs.

Selling Advertising Space

You can directly sell ad space on your website to businesses. This gives you more control over the ads that appear on your site.

Target specific businesses: Identify companies that would be a good fit for your audience.
Offer different ad sizes and placements: Provide options for advertisers based on their needs and budget.
Set clear rates and contracts: Be professional in your dealings with advertisers.

Freemium Model

Here's an idea that blends the best of both worlds: Offer some content or services for free and charge for premium features.

Offer a free tier: Give people a taste of what you have to offer with a free version of your product or service.
Upgrade to premium: Offer premium features, like more storage, advanced tools, or exclusive content, to those who pay.

Donating

Sometimes, the best things in life are free. If you create valuable content or services, your audience might want to show their appreciation through donations.

Set up a donation button: Platforms like PayPal or Stripe allow you to add donation buttons to your website.
Offer incentives: Encourage donations by offering rewards, like exclusive content or early access to new features.

Tips for Monetizing Your Website

Remember, grandma's always got a few extra tips up her sleeve!

Focus on quality content: The foundation of any successful monetization strategy is great content that your audience loves.

Build a loyal audience: The more engaged your audience is, the more valuable your website becomes.

Be patient and consistent: Monetization takes time. Don't get discouraged if you don't see results overnight. Keep creating great content and promoting your website, and the money will follow.

Choose the right methods: Not all monetization strategies work for every website. Experiment and find what works best for you.

Stay ethical: Always be transparent with your audience about how you make money. Don't try to trick them or mislead them.

Remember, grandma's always here to cheer you on! Building a website is a journey. Enjoy the process, learn along the way, and don't be afraid to try new things. With a little creativity and a lot of hard work, you can turn your website into a valuable asset that can generate income or support your business goals. Now go out there and build something amazing!

Inspiring Case Studies

The world of website building is filled with stories of ordinary people who have achieved extraordinary things. It's a journey of exploration, creativity, and endless possibilities, and many have taken the leap, turning their passions and dreams into online realities. Let's delve into a few inspiring case studies that showcase the power of beginner-friendly website building.

The Retired Teacher's Culinary Adventures

Meet Mary, a retired teacher who always had a passion for cooking. With the extra time on her hands, she decided to share her culinary creations with the world. She had no prior experience in web development, but armed with a desire to connect with others who share her love of food, she embarked on her website building journey.

Mary chose a user-friendly website builder, allowing her to focus on the content rather than technical intricacies. She started with a simple design, showcasing her recipes in a clear and appealing way. Through the platform's intuitive interface, she added eye-catching images and videos, bringing her recipes to life. As her website gained traction, she began sharing her stories and experiences, connecting with readers through her warmth and genuineness. Her website became a hub for food lovers, a space where she could share her culinary passion and build a community around her recipes.

What started as a simple desire to share her love of cooking turned into a vibrant online platform. Mary's website attracted a loyal following of readers eager to learn from her culinary expertise. She even launched a newsletter, allowing her to connect with her audience on a more personal level. This testament to her commitment and dedication to sharing her passion shows that with a little effort and determination, anyone can create a successful website, regardless of prior experience.

The Travel Blogger's Journey of Exploration

Mark, an avid traveler, always dreamt of sharing his adventures with the world. He yearned to inspire others to explore new destinations, but felt overwhelmed by the technical aspects of website creation. With the encouragement of his friends, he decided to give it a try. He opted for a website builder that offered a range of travel-specific templates, making it easy to create a visually appealing site that reflected his adventurous spirit.

Mark's website became a captivating blend of vibrant photography, engaging stories, and practical travel tips. He meticulously crafted blog posts that transported readers to exotic locations, sharing his experiences in an authentic and relatable manner. With each post, he incorporated maps, itineraries, and local recommendations, making his site a valuable resource for aspiring travelers. As his readership grew, Mark embraced the power of social media, sharing his blog posts and captivating photographs, further amplifying his reach.

Mark's success demonstrates that creating a successful website doesn't require advanced technical skills. With a little creativity and passion, anyone can share their adventures with the world, inspiring others to travel and explore.

The Small Business Owner's Digital Transformation

Sarah, a talented florist, longed to expand her small business's reach. She had always relied on word-of-mouth referrals but realized the potential of online platforms to attract new customers. However, she felt intimidated by the complexities of website building, fearing it was beyond her capabilities.

Sarah decided to take a leap of faith and explore the possibilities of WordPress. She found a user-friendly theme specifically designed for businesses, allowing her to showcase her floral arrangements and services with stunning visuals. With the help of online tutorials and support forums, she learned to customize her website, adding features like a contact form and an online booking system. Sarah's website became a virtual storefront, allowing customers to browse her floral collection, learn about her services, and conveniently place orders.

Sarah's journey highlights how a website can transform a small business, turning it into a thriving online entity. Her dedication to learning and adapting to the ever-evolving world of web development demonstrates that even those with limited technical skills can embrace digital platforms to grow their businesses.

These inspiring case studies are just a glimpse into the countless stories of individuals who have successfully built websites, sharing their passions, connecting with others, and realizing their online aspirations. They showcase the power of user-friendly website platforms and demonstrate that with a little determination and guidance, anyone can create a website that makes a difference.

Beyond the Case Studies: Common Pitfalls and Lessons Learned

While the stories of Mary, Mark, and Sarah paint a picture of success, the journey of website building isn't always a smooth one. Along the way, there are challenges and pitfalls that every beginner needs to be aware of.

1. The Overwhelming Nature of Choices:

The first hurdle many beginners encounter is the overwhelming number of choices they face. From selecting a domain name and hosting service to choosing a website builder or theme, the initial steps can feel daunting. It's easy to get caught up in the myriad options and lose sight of the bigger picture.

Lesson Learned: Focus on the essentials. Start with a clear vision of what you want to achieve with your website and prioritize those elements that will help you accomplish your goals. Don't feel pressured to incorporate every bells and whistles. Keep it simple and scalable, allowing you to add features as your needs grow.

2. The Fear of Technology:

For many, the fear of technology remains a significant barrier. The thought of learning coding, troubleshooting technical issues, or managing website security can be intimidating. This fear can hold them back from taking the plunge and venturing into the world of website building.

Lesson Learned: Embrace the learning process. Technology can be a powerful tool, but it's also constantly evolving. Don't be afraid to ask for help, explore online tutorials, and join supportive communities. Remember, every website builder and platform has its own learning curve, and with patience and persistence, you can master the necessary skills.

3. The Lack of Content Consistency:

Once the website is launched, a common pitfall is the lack of consistent content creation. This can lead to a stagnant site with outdated information, diminishing its appeal to visitors.

Lesson Learned: Develop a content strategy. Create a plan for publishing regular content, whether it's blog posts, articles, or updates. This could include a content calendar, allowing you to stay organized and consistently provide fresh information.

4. The Neglect of SEO Optimization:

Often, beginners overlook the importance of search engine optimization (SEO). They focus on creating beautiful visuals and compelling content but fail to ensure their website is visible to their target audience.

Lesson Learned: Optimize for search engines. Invest time in learning SEO basics. Use relevant keywords in your content, create descriptive meta descriptions, and optimize your images. By making your website search engine-friendly, you increase the chances of attracting more visitors and achieving your website goals.

5. The Absence of Analytics:

While it's exciting to launch a website, it's equally important to track its performance. Many beginners fail to implement analytics tools, leaving them in the dark about their website's engagement and effectiveness.

Lesson Learned: Track your website's performance. Integrate analytics tools to gather data about your visitors, their behavior, and your website's overall effectiveness. This information will help you identify areas for improvement and adjust your content strategy accordingly.

The Future of Your Website: Embrace the Journey

The world of website building is constantly evolving, with new technologies and trends emerging all the time. It's a journey of constant learning, exploration, and adaptation. As you navigate this digital landscape, remember to:

Stay curious: Embrace the ever-changing landscape of website building and technology. Explore new platforms, tools, and techniques.
Experiment and iterate: Don't be afraid to try new things and adjust your website based on your learnings. There's no one-size-fits-all approach, so find what works best for you.
Connect and learn from others: Join online communities, participate in forums, and engage with other website builders. Sharing knowledge and experiences can accelerate your learning and growth.

Your website is a reflection of your vision, your passion, and your desire to connect with the world. Embrace the journey of website building, learn from your experiences, and never stop exploring the possibilities of the digital landscape. The stories of Mary, Mark, and Sarah prove that with a little determination and a whole lot of heart, you can create a website that makes a difference in your own unique way.

Lessons Learned and Common Pitfalls

Building a website is like embarking on a thrilling adventure. You'll encounter unexpected twists and turns, moments of triumph, and perhaps even a few setbacks along the way. Learning from the experiences of others can provide valuable insights and help you navigate the journey more smoothly.

Lesson 1: The Importance of a Clear Plan: Just like a well-crafted recipe, a successful website needs a clear plan. Before you dive into the world of code and design, take some time to define your goals. Ask yourself: What is the purpose of your website? Who is your target audience? What kind of content will you create? Having a roadmap in place will help you stay focused and avoid getting lost in the vast ocean of online possibilities.

Lesson 2: Master the Basics: Learning the fundamentals is crucial, especially when you're starting out. This means understanding basic web design principles, like typography, color palettes, and layout. It also involves getting familiar with common web development terms and tools. While it's tempting to jump into advanced features, building a solid foundation will ensure a stronger and more stable website.

Lesson 3: The Power of Content: Content is king. Your website's content should be engaging, informative, and relevant to your audience. Take the time to write well-crafted articles, create compelling videos, or share beautiful images. Think about how you can provide value to your visitors, whether it's through entertainment, education, or inspiration.

Lesson 4: Embrace SEO: SEO, or Search Engine Optimization, is the art of making your website visible to search engines. By incorporating SEO best practices, you'll improve your chances of ranking higher in search results. This means using relevant keywords, optimizing images, and creating high-quality content. Remember, a website that's not found is a website that's not visited.

Lesson 5: The Importance of Security: Security is paramount in the digital world. Just like you lock your doors at home, you need to take steps to protect your website from cyber threats. This includes using strong passwords, regularly updating software, and being aware of common security vulnerabilities. Neglecting security measures can lead to data breaches, lost information, and a damaged reputation.

Lesson 6: Be Patient and Persistent: Building a successful website takes time and effort. Don't expect to become a web development guru overnight. Be patient with yourself, embrace the learning process, and celebrate every milestone. There will be challenges along the way, but with persistence and a willingness to learn, you'll achieve your goals.

Pitfall 1: The Allure of Over-Complexity: It's easy to get caught up in the desire for a flashy, feature-packed website. But remember, simplicity often reigns supreme. Avoid overwhelming visitors with too much information or too many distracting elements. Focus on creating a clean, user-friendly interface that clearly conveys your message.

Pitfall 2: Neglecting the User Experience: Design your website with your visitors in mind. Consider how they will navigate your site, what information they're looking for, and what actions you want them to take. Don't make them struggle to find what they need. Aim to create an intuitive, enjoyable experience that encourages them to stay and explore.

Pitfall 3: Ignoring Mobile Optimization: In today's mobile-first world, it's essential to ensure your website is optimized for viewing on smartphones and tablets. A website that's not mobile-friendly can be difficult to navigate and frustrating for users. Make sure your website is responsive and adaptable to different screen sizes.

Pitfall 4: Underestimating the Importance of Maintenance: A website is not a set-and-forget endeavor. Regular updates, backups, and security checks are crucial for keeping your website running smoothly and securely. Neglecting maintenance can lead to downtime, security breaches, and even data loss.

Pitfall 5: The Fear of Failure: Don't let the fear of failure hold you back. Mistakes are an inevitable part of the learning process. Embrace them as opportunities to learn and grow. Remember, every successful website started with a single step, a single line of code, a single idea.

Real-Life Success Stories: The world is full of inspiring individuals who have built incredible websites from scratch. Take, for example, Sarah, a retired teacher who started a blog about gardening. She knew nothing about web design, but her passion for her subject and her willingness to learn led her to create a website that attracted a loyal community of gardening enthusiasts. Sarah's website is a testament to the power of dedication, perseverance, and the joy of sharing your passion with the world.

Final Thoughts: Building a website is a rewarding experience that empowers you to create your own corner of the online world. Embrace the challenges, celebrate your successes, and don't be afraid to ask for help when you need it. With the right guidance, the right tools, and a touch of creativity, you can turn your website dreams into a reality.

Resources and Further Learning

The world of web development is vast and ever-evolving, with new technologies and tools emerging all the time. While this book has equipped you with the foundational knowledge and practical skills to build your own website, it's just the beginning of your journey. The beauty of the internet is that it's a boundless source of information and resources for continuous learning and growth.

Think of this book as your trusty guidebook, but remember that there are countless other resources and communities out there waiting to support your ongoing exploration. Let's dive into some invaluable avenues for further learning and expanding your website building expertise:

Online Courses and Tutorials:

The internet is overflowing with online courses and tutorials designed for aspiring web developers of all levels. Platforms like Coursera, Udemy, Skillshare, and Khan Academy offer a wide array of courses covering various aspects of web development, from coding fundamentals to specialized topics like website design, SEO optimization, and marketing.

Take advantage of free trials or discounted offers to explore courses that pique your interest. You can learn at your own pace, revisit modules as needed, and engage with instructors and fellow learners through online forums and Q&A sessions. Remember, practice makes perfect, so actively participate in the learning process by completing assignments, building projects, and engaging in hands-on exercises.

WordPress Communities and Forums:

WordPress, the popular content management system, boasts a vibrant and supportive community of users, developers, and enthusiasts.

WordPress.org Support Forums: The official WordPress.org support forums are a treasure trove of information and assistance. You can search for answers to specific questions or post your own queries to receive help from experienced WordPress users.

WordPress Meetups: Consider attending local WordPress meetups or online events to connect with other WordPress enthusiasts. These gatherings provide an excellent opportunity to share knowledge, network, and gain valuable insights from experienced users.

WordPress Blogs and Podcasts: Numerous blogs and podcasts are dedicated to WordPress news, tips, and tutorials. Subscribe to those that align with your interests and learning goals. These platforms offer a continuous stream of updates, insights, and practical advice to enhance your WordPress skills.

Web Development Books:

While this book serves as a great starting point, there's a vast world of web development books out there to deepen your knowledge and expand your skillset. Explore books covering specific topics such as:

Front-End Development: Learn about HTML, CSS, and JavaScript – the languages that define the structure, style, and interactivity of your website.

Back-End Development: Delve into server-side technologies like PHP, Python, or Ruby to understand how your website interacts with databases and other systems.

SEO Optimization: Enhance your website's visibility in search engine results pages (SERPs) with books dedicated to SEO strategies and techniques.
Web Design Principles: Discover the principles of visual design to create aesthetically pleasing and user-friendly websites.
Content Marketing: Learn the art of crafting compelling content that resonates with your target audience and drives engagement.

Coding Boot Camps:

For a more immersive and structured learning experience, consider enrolling in a coding boot camp. These intensive programs offer a hands-on approach to web development, combining classroom instruction with real-world projects. Boot camps typically last for a few months and equip you with the skills and portfolio to land a job as a web developer.

Learning Resources and Tools:

Codecademy: A popular online platform that provides interactive coding lessons across various programming languages, including HTML, CSS, and JavaScript.
FreeCodeCamp: A non-profit organization offering a comprehensive curriculum for web development skills, including front-end, back-end, and data science.
W3Schools: A comprehensive online resource for web development tutorials, reference materials, and interactive examples covering HTML, CSS, JavaScript, and more.
Mozilla Developer Network (MDN): A wealth of documentation, tutorials, and reference materials for web developers, maintained by the Mozilla Foundation.
Stack Overflow: An online community where programmers can ask and answer questions, share knowledge, and collaborate on coding challenges.

Remember, Learning Is a Continuous Journey:

Web development is a dynamic field that constantly evolves. Embrace the ongoing journey of learning, staying up-to-date with the latest trends, and exploring new tools and technologies. The internet provides an unparalleled platform for continuous learning, allowing you to connect with a global community of developers, access valuable resources, and push your web development skills to new heights.

Embrace the Community:

Don't underestimate the power of community support. Engage with fellow learners, ask questions, and share your experiences. You'll find that the web development community is a welcoming and supportive environment where everyone is eager to help each other succeed.

As you continue your journey, remember the joy of creation and the satisfaction of building something meaningful from scratch. Your website is a reflection of your vision, creativity, and dedication. Embrace the challenges, celebrate your successes, and enjoy the rewarding experience of bringing your ideas to life online.

The Future of Your Website

The world of the internet is constantly evolving, just like everything else, and your website needs to stay up-to-date to keep pace. It's exciting to think about the possibilities, isn't it? Imagine a website that adapts to your visitor's preferences, anticipates their needs, and even engages in conversations with them! Sounds like something out of a sci-fi movie, right? Well, that's not so far-fetched anymore.

One of the most exciting developments in website technology is the rise of **Artificial Intelligence (AI)** . AI can be used to automate tasks like content creation, customer service, and even design. Imagine AI-powered chatbots that answer your website visitors' questions, personalize their experience, and suggest relevant content. You can even use AI to analyze data and understand your audience's preferences better, allowing you to optimize your website and tailor it to their needs.

Another trend that's gaining momentum is **Voice Search** . More and more people are using their voice to search for information online. You can optimize your website for voice search by using natural language and long-tail keywords, making it easier for voice assistants like Siri or Alexa to understand your content and provide relevant results.

Augmented Reality (AR) and Virtual Reality (VR) are also making their way into the world of websites. Imagine showcasing your products in a virtual storefront, allowing customers to try them on or interact with them in a virtual space. This immersive experience can create a more engaging and memorable experience for your visitors.

The future of your website is bright! By staying informed about emerging trends and incorporating them into your strategy, you can ensure that your website remains relevant, engaging, and impactful. Don't be afraid to experiment, and remember that the journey is just as important as the destination. Just like you've learned to navigate the world of websites, you can continue learning and adapting as the technology evolves.

Let's explore some specific examples of how these future trends might impact your website. Imagine you're running a small online bookstore. You could use AI to analyze customer purchase history and suggest personalized recommendations for each visitor. You could create a voice-activated ordering system, allowing customers to place orders by simply speaking to their smart devices. And imagine offering virtual tours of your bookstore, allowing customers to browse your collection in a virtual environment.

These are just a few examples of how future trends can enhance your website's functionality and user experience. The possibilities are endless, limited only by our imagination.

The Future of Website Design

Beyond the technological advancements, website design is also evolving. Gone are the days of clunky websites with long blocks of text and cluttered layouts. Modern websites are designed to be clean, intuitive, and mobile-friendly.

Minimalism will continue to be a dominant design trend. Websites with clean layouts, simple typography, and a focus on high-quality visuals will create a more enjoyable experience for visitors. This approach allows users to easily find the information they need and reduces distractions.

Interactive Elements will become even more commonplace. Websites that engage visitors through interactive elements like quizzes, polls, games, and animations are more likely to keep them hooked. These elements can also be used to gather data about user preferences and behavior, helping you to better understand your audience and optimize your site.

Personalization is another key trend. Websites will become increasingly personalized, tailoring content and recommendations to individual user preferences. This personalized approach can create a more engaging and relevant experience for visitors, leading to higher conversion rates and greater customer satisfaction.

The future of website design is about creating seamless, intuitive, and personalized experiences for users. By embracing these trends, you can ensure that your website remains visually appealing, engaging, and effective.

Keeping Up with the Times

The key to staying ahead in the ever-changing world of websites is continuous learning and adaptation. You don't have to be a tech expert to understand these trends and how they can benefit your website. Many online resources and platforms provide valuable information and tutorials to help you stay up-to-date.

One of the best ways to stay informed is to follow reputable websites and blogs that focus on website design and development. You can also attend online workshops and webinars to learn about the latest trends and techniques.

Remember, the journey of building and maintaining a website is an ongoing process. It's a continuous learning experience that requires curiosity, adaptability, and a willingness to embrace change.

So, don't be afraid to experiment and explore new possibilities. Let your website be a reflection of your creativity and passion, and don't be afraid to adapt and evolve with the ever-changing landscape of the internet. After all, just like a grandparent who constantly learns and grows, you too can keep your website fresh, relevant, and engaging.

Encouragement and Next Steps

So, you've reached the end of our journey together. You've taken the first steps, learned the ropes, and now you have a website that reflects your passions, your business, or your personal story. Congratulations! Building a website can feel like a daunting task, but you've done it. You've become a website builder!

As you continue to grow your website, remember that this is an ongoing process. The world of technology is constantly evolving, so staying informed and adaptable is key. Don't be afraid to experiment, try new things, and adapt your approach as you learn. You'll discover new strategies, tools, and trends that can help you refine your website and achieve your goals.

Here are some key takeaways and next steps to keep in mind:

1. Keep Learning and Growing:

The world of website development is a dynamic one. New technologies, platforms, and techniques emerge all the time. Embrace continuous learning. Explore resources such as online courses, blogs, podcasts, and communities where you can stay updated on the latest trends.

Online Courses: Platforms like Coursera, Udemy, and Skillshare offer comprehensive courses on web development, WordPress, SEO, and various other relevant topics. These courses can provide structured learning paths with hands-on exercises.

Blogs and Websites: There are countless blogs and websites dedicated to web development, WordPress, and digital marketing. Some popular options include WPEngine's blog, Yoast SEO blog, and Moz blog. These platforms offer valuable insights, tutorials, and best practices.

Podcasts: Listen to podcasts like "The Web Developer Podcast," "WordPress Tavern," and "Search Engine Journal Podcast" to stay updated on the latest industry news and trends.

Communities: Engage with online communities like WordPress forums, Reddit communities (r/wordpress, r/webdev), and Facebook groups. These platforms offer spaces to ask questions, share experiences, and learn from others.

2. Don't Be Afraid to Experiment:

Once you've built your website, don't be afraid to tinker with it, try out new plugins, explore different themes, and experiment with various design elements. You'll discover what works best for you and your audience.

Plugins: WordPress has a vast library of plugins that offer various functionalities, from SEO optimization to social media integration. Experiment with different plugins to see how they can enhance your website.

Themes: Try out different WordPress themes to find one that perfectly matches your brand and content. You can also customize your existing theme to add your personal touch.

Design Elements: Play with different fonts, colors, images, and layouts to find a design that is visually appealing and effectively communicates your message.

3. Prioritize User Experience:

Always focus on creating a positive user experience. This means making your website easy to navigate, visually appealing, and fast-loading.

User-Friendly Navigation: Ensure that your website is easy to navigate with clear menus, intuitive links, and a logical structure.

Visual Appeal: Utilize high-quality images, visually appealing layouts, and a consistent brand identity to create a visually engaging experience.

Speed Optimization: Optimize your website for speed by compressing images, minimizing code, and choosing a reliable hosting provider.

4. Build Relationships with Your Audience:

Your website is not just a static platform; it's a way to connect with your audience.

Engagement: Encourage interaction through comments, social media sharing, and email subscriptions.

Community Building: Create a sense of community by responding to comments, engaging in discussions, and organizing events.

5. Stay Consistent and Persistent:

Building a successful website takes time and effort. Consistency is key.

Regular Updates: Update your website regularly with fresh content, news, and updates.

Promote Your Website: Use social media, email marketing, and other strategies to promote your website and drive traffic.

Track Your Progress: Use website analytics to track your website's performance and identify areas for improvement.

6. Measure Your Success:

Defining your success metrics is crucial. Determine what constitutes success for your website.

Website Traffic: Track your website's traffic using Google Analytics.

Engagement Metrics: Monitor metrics like bounce rate, time on site, and page views.

Conversion Rates: If your website has a call-to-action, track conversion rates.

Social Media Engagement: Monitor engagement on your social media platforms.

7. Don't Be Afraid to Ask for Help:

There are countless resources available to help you along the way. Don't hesitate to seek assistance from online communities, forums, or website development professionals.

Online Forums: WordPress forums and other online communities are great places to ask questions and get help from experienced users.

Website Development Professionals: If you encounter complex issues or need specialized assistance, consider hiring a professional web developer or designer.

8. Have Fun and Enjoy the Process:

Building a website is a rewarding experience. Enjoy the journey of creating something from scratch, connecting with your audience, and sharing your story with the world.

Remember, you've come a long way. You've learned valuable skills, and you're now equipped to navigate the exciting world of website building. Keep exploring, keep learning, and keep creating. I'm confident you'll achieve great things!

Acknowledgments

First and foremost, I want to express my deepest gratitude to all the amazing web developers who have generously shared their knowledge and expertise over the years. From online forums to insightful blog posts, your guidance has been invaluable in my own journey of learning and growth.

To all the aspiring website builders out there, I hope this book inspires you to embrace the world of online creation. Remember, anyone can build a website, and your journey begins with the first step!

Appendix

This appendix provides additional resources and tools that might be helpful in your website-building journey.

List of Popular Website Builders: A curated list of popular website builders with brief descriptions and links to their websites.
Essential WordPress Plugins: A comprehensive list of essential WordPress plugins for security, functionality, and user experience.
Free Stock Photo Resources: Links to websites that offer high-quality free stock photos for use on your website.
Web Development Tools: A collection of useful web development tools, such as code editors, website testing platforms, and SEO analysis tools.

Glossary

Domain Name: The unique address of your website on the internet (e.g., www.example.com).
Web Hosting: The service that provides storage space and resources for your website to exist online.
WordPress: A popular content management system (CMS) used for building websites and blogs.
Theme: A pre-designed template that defines the overall appearance and layout of your website.
Plugin: An extension that adds specific features or functionality to your WordPress website.
SEO (Search Engine Optimization): Techniques used to improve your website's visibility in search engine results.
Content Management System (CMS): A software application used to manage website content and functionality.
Analytics: Tools that track and analyze website traffic and user behavior.

References

For the Beginner:

- "Website Building for Dummies": A straightforward, easy-to-understand guide with step-by-step instructions and simple language.
- "Websites for Everyone: Your Beginner's Guide": Focuses on user-friendly platforms and tools, minimizing technical jargon.
- "From Zero to Website: A Practical Guide for Beginners": Emphasizes building a website from scratch, starting with essential concepts and then progressing to more advanced features.

For the Experienced Web Developer:

- "Advanced Web Development: Mastering Modern Techniques": A comprehensive guide to advanced topics like server-side programming, databases, and complex front-end frameworks.
- "Best Practices for Building Scalable Websites": Focuses on building efficient, high-performance websites that can handle large traffic and complex data.
- "Building Secure Websites: A Developer's Guide to Security": Covers essential security practices and vulnerabilities, teaching developers how to build safe and protected websites.

For the Creative:

- "Designing Beautiful Websites: A Guide to Visual Storytelling": Emphasizes design principles, visual hierarchy, and user experience, focusing on building aesthetically pleasing websites.
- "The Art of Web Design: From Inspiration to Implementation": Combines design theory with practical skills, inspiring readers to create unique and innovative websites.
- "Website Design for Small Businesses: How to Stand Out Online": Provides tailored advice and strategies for building successful websites for small businesses, emphasizing branding and online presence.

For the Entrepreneur:

- "Building a Website to Launch Your Business": Focuses on using a website to attract customers, generate leads, and promote products or services.
- "Website Marketing Strategies: From Content to Conversion": Provides actionable strategies for driving traffic to a website, converting visitors, and building an online audience.
- "Building Your Brand Online: From Website to Social Media": Explores how to leverage a website as part of a broader online branding strategy, integrating with social media and other online platforms.

Author Biography

Tracy McCartney has been a passionate web developer for over 10 years, with a particular focus on helping beginners navigate the world of website creation. With a friendly and approachable teaching style, she aims to empower individuals of all ages to build their own websites with confidence.

www.ingramcontent.com/pod-product-compliance
Lightning Source LLC
Chambersburg PA
CBHW071452220526
45472CB00003B/768